Student Companion

for

Wood's

Interpersonal Communication
Everyday Encounters
Fifth Edition

Debi L. Iba
Texas Christian University

Julia T. Wood
University of North Carolina, Chapel Hill

THOMSON

★ TM

WADSWORTH

Australia • Brazil • Canada • Mexico • Singapore • Spain • United Kingdom • United States

Printer: Thomson West

ISBN 0-495-13094-X

Cover Images: Clockwise from top: © John Feingersh/ CORBIS; © Franco Vogt/CORBIS; © Royalty-Free CORBIS

Thomson Higher Education
10 Davis Drive
Belmont, CA 94002-3098
USA

For more information about our products, contact us at:
Thomson Learning Academic Resource Center
1-800-423-0563

For permission to use material from this text or product, submit a request online at
http://www.thomsonrights.com.
Any additional questions about permissions can be submitted by email to
thomsonrights@thomson.com.

Preface

Welcome to the *Student Companion to Interpersonal Communication–Everyday Encounters*. My name is Debi Iba (pronounced *eye-buh*). I'm not the author of your main textbook, but I when I was invited to revise the *Student Companion* for the 5th edition I readily agreed. The main text is very engaging in that it speaks in the author's own voice. The *Student Companion* offers you the opportunity to speak in your voice in response to many of the main points.

I teach at Texas Christian University in Fort Worth, Texas, and I've been teaching interpersonal communication concepts for many years. The students in my Interpersonal Communication class tell me that this course is much more than learning to communicate effectively—it's about learning to live effectively. I agree completely. My spouse and I have been married nearly 20 years and we have two sons in our family. Our busy schedules take us to all points in the area, and effective communication is what keeps us all connected and accountable.

The Interpersonal Communication course has evolved and changed a great deal since I started teaching, particularly with the explosion of Internet communication. Email and chat rooms keep us connected with family, friends, and coworkers whether they are across the hall or around the world. We meet people on discussion boards, and through newsgroups and blogs. Electronic communication—whether it is text-messaging, instant-messaging, Internet, or email —has become an integral part of how we create, maintain, and dissolve our interpersonal relationships.

When I was an undergraduate at Missouri State University, I enrolled in a communication course and found my career calling. I had some terrific professors, and upon graduation I promptly enrolled in the graduate program in Communication Studies. I found the courses to be highly interactive, and I perpetuate this in my own courses today. This kind of interactive approach to interpersonal communication is evident in Julia Wood's *Interpersonal Communication—Everyday Encounters* textbook which is the primary reason I was am so delighted to be involved with this new edition. This theme of encouraging active participation has been carried through from the first edition of this *Student Companion*, through the second edition (by Michelle T. Violanti, the lead author), the third edition (by Walter John Carl, the lead author), the fourth edition (by Stephanie Coopman, the lead author), and now this fifth edition. As all of us have worked on this *Student Companion*, we have tried to make you an active part of the process rather than a passive recipient of information.

Objectives of the Course and Textbook

An introductory course in interpersonal communication raises your aware of the theories and research that provide the foundations for study in this field. In addition, successfully completing a class in interpersonal communication increases communication competence in your personal and professional lives. Further, the *Interpersonal Communication—Everyday Encounters* textbook pays significant attention to social trends, issues, and concerns that affect how you communicate in 21st century Western culture. These trends include cultural diversity, communication technologies, and timely social issues such as workplace communication, long distance friendships, safe sex practices in an era of HIV/AIDS, and violence between intimates.

Objectives and Format of this Student Companion

The *Student Companion* facilitates your understanding of the theories, concepts, and research discussed in the textbook, and provides you with an opportunity to put these ideas into practice. In the past, many of the student-oriented textbook accompaniments we have seen present a chapter outline in the same terms you may or may not have understood while reading the chapter, ask you to define some terms or answer some practice test items, and provide some "busy work" activities/exercises that your instructor may or may not require. In an attempt to make this companion more user-friendly and beneficial to you, we have included the following sections for each chapter to correspond to the textbook chapters.

Chapter Content–These outline frameworks highlight the information contained in each textbook chapter. Where they diverge from what you have seen previously is that they ask you to complete sections of the outline in your own words and also ask you to generate personal examples to illustrate the concepts. After reading the textbook chapter, close the textbook and see how much of the outline you can complete (this is a good way to test your initial comprehension of the material). We have found in our teaching that students are very good at memorizing the examples or definitions provided in the textbook, but if we ask the question in a different way or ask them to apply the material to a different type of situation, they are unsure at best and lost at worst. Having your own examples should help you determine how well you understand/comprehend the material and aid your ability to use this information in your relationships once you leave this classroom.

Additional Vocabulary–These are terms that were mentioned in the textbook and not highlighted for examples in the chapter content section. Again, rather than asking you to write out the definition, we ask you for a personal example to illustrate each concept. Think about it: If you have a personal example, you should be able to go back and generate a definition or pick out a definition for each term on an exam. Personal examples also illustrate the overlapping nature of concepts involved in interpersonal communication.

Key Concepts– In this section, we have included all the bold-faced terms from the textbook in list form. We provide you with this list so that you can see all the key terms in one place, rather than having to pick them out in the "Chapter Content" and "Additional Vocabulary" sections.

Activities–There are a number of activities that fortify and extend the textbook's coverage. Some of the activities invite you to reflect on your own experiences as a communicator while others provide you with ways of developing greater skills in communicating with and analyzing the communication of others. All activities are broken down into individual, partner, group, ethnographic (that is, where you go to participate or observe a situation, and/or interview people), and Internet or InfoTrac-College Edition (explained below). A Grid at the beginning of each Activity section groups each exercise. Further, all the Activities are all printed on perforated pages so you can remove them for easy carrying and/or turning in as class assignments.

Web Sites–The number of web sites devoted to interpersonal communication have increased considerably in the past few years. When the second edition of this book was written (in 1999), one search engine found 54,000 web pages on the topic of "interpersonal communication." In 2003 a Google search identified nearly 600,000 web pages related to interpersonal communication. Two years later, Google found nearly 1.8 million web pages on the topic (go ahead, see for yourself!). Clearly, it is not practical for you to spend your time weeding through all of these to find the one that will be beneficial, so we have done that for you (though feel free to search for your own too!). After many hours in front of the computer screen, we have narrowed these down to a handful of useful sites for each chapter's content. Please understand that we have no control over when people create or remove their pages so it is possible that you will encounter some addresses that no longer exist. That is one of the challenges of working with this particular technology. In addition to the URL address, we have provided you with the name of the site, the developer, and a brief description.

InfoTrac-College Edition– InfoTrac-College Edition is a world-class online library that you can use to learn more about content covered in each chapter and to conduct your own research. Some of the activities ask you to do further research on a particular topic by using InfoTrac and then to share the results of your research with others in your class.

Self-Tests–So that you can check your understanding of each chapter's content, there are sample test items. Taking the sample tests for each chapter is another way of checking your understanding and focusing your study time to make it as productive and rewarding as possible. An answer key is provided at the end of this manual with page numbers of the textbook where you can find more information about the question.

Personal Reflections–These are suggested topics if you are required or decide to keep a journal during the course.

We hope that you find the *Student Companion* useful in your study of interpersonal communication. If you have any questions or comments, we would like to hear them (both positive and constructive criticism). You can reach us at the following addresses:

Debi L. Iba
Department of Communication Studies
Texas Christian University
Box 298045
Fort Worth, Texas 76129
d.iba@tcu.edu

Julia T. Wood
Department of Communication Studies
CB#3285, Bingham Hall
University of North Carolina
Chapel Hill, North Carolina 27516
JWood1@email.unc.edu

Have a wonderful interpersonal communication experience!

Debi L. Iba

Julia T. Wood

Table of Contents

Chapter 1:   A First Look at Interpersonal Communication

I.   Communication meets many of the basic human needs that Abraham Maslow identified.

A.   Physical needs help us survive. An example of a time when I used communication to achieve this need is _____

_____

_____

B.   Safety needs protect us from harm. An example of a time when I used communication to meet this need is _____   _____

_____

_____

C.   Belonging needs connect us to others. An example of a time when I used communication to meet this need is _____

_____

_____

D.   Self-esteem needs indicate that we are valued by/important to others. An example of a time when I used communication to meet this need is _____

_____

_____

E.   Self-actualization needs are experiences that help us reach our fullest individual potential. An example of a time when I used communication to achieve this need is _____

_____

_____

II.   Interpersonal communication is not defined by the number of people in the interaction or the context in which the communication occurs.

    A.   Models help us understand the historical roots from which our current views of communication grew.

        1.   Linear models treated communication as a one-way process in which one person transmitted a message to another person.

            a.   Laswell's model answered the following five questions:

(1)_____

(2)_____

(3)_____

(4)_____

(5)_____

            b.   Shannon and Weaver's model illustrated how a message goes from a source to a destination and added the feature of noise. Draw a picture of their telephone model here:

            c.   Two problems with these linear models were that they:

(1)_____

(2)_____

2.   Interactive models addressed the weakness in linear models, which viewed listeners as passive recipients, by adding feedback to the communication process.

   a.   The interactive model recognized that communicators are both creators and interpreters of messages. The creation and interpretation processes are based upon a person's field of experience. Draw a picture of the model here:

   b.   Even with this advance, two linear model problems remained:
   (1)_____
   (2)_____

3.   Transactional models recognize the dynamic (changing) nature of communication. Draw a picture of the transactional model here:

B.   There are three levels of communication.

    1.   <u>I-It communication</u> occurs when we treat others like objects or non-humans. An example of a time when I used I-It communication is_____

_____

    2.   <u>I-You communication</u> occurs when we recognize the other as a person and treat her or him based upon a social role he or she occupies. This constitutes the majority of our communication. An example of a time when I engaged in I-You communication is _____

_____

    3.   <u>I-Thou communication</u> occurs when we recognize and understand an individual's unique characteristics as well as open ourselves completely to this person. An example of a time when I engaged in I-Thou communication is _____

_____

C.   Interpersonal communication is a selective, systemic, unique, and ongoing process of interaction between individuals who reflect and build personal knowledge of one another and create shared meanings.

    1.   Interpersonal communication occurs within a variety of systems and contexts.

        a.   The situation, time, people, culture, and personal histories all affect the way we create and interpret messages.

        b.   Noise is anything that distracts our attention so they we fail to give our undivided attention to an interaction. An example of physical noise that distracted me today is _____

_____

_____

    c.   An example of psychological noise that distracted me today is_____

             _____

             _____

    d.   An example of semantic noise that distracted me today is _____

             _____

             _____

    e.   An example of physiological noise that distracted me today is_____

             _____

             _____

2.   Each new relationship we build is different from all of the ones that came before it. No two interpersonal relationships are exactly alike.

3.   Interpersonal communication evolves over time, is affected by our past, and influences our future.

4.   Because interpersonal communication is an interaction, both parties create and interpret messages, are responsible for the communication's effectiveness, and must get to know each other personally.

5.   Attaching meanings to the words we exchange requires knowledge of the other person and the relationship in which we are engaged.

    a.   <u>Content meanings</u> are the definitions we could look up in a dictionary. A content meaning for "You're bad" would be _____

             _____

        b.   <u>Relational meanings</u> are the understandings we have because of the connection we have to the other person/people involved in the interaction. A relational meaning for "You're bad" might be

_____

_____

III.   Our definition of interpersonal communication implies basic principles.

    A.   We cannot avoid communicating when we are with other people.

    B.   Because communication is irreversible, we can never take back what we say or do and we always have an impact on the person/people with whom we are interacting.

    C.   Because interpersonal communication affects us and others, ethical considerations are always parts of our interactions. Ethical issues concern what is right and what is wrong in our interactions with others. An example of a time when I made an ethical choice my communication is _____

_____

_____

    D.   Meanings are not in words or actions alone, but rather in the participants' interpretations of those words and actions.

    E.   Metacommunication is how we let others know, both verbally and nonverbally, about whether the way we are interacting is helping us create shared understanding. It also helps us express how we feel about our interactions with our friends and/or partners.

    F.   Interpersonal communication is the primary way we build, refine, and transform relationships. A time when I constructed a shared future with a friend or intimate is

_____

_____

G. Interpersonal communication does not solve all problems. An example of a problem in my life that communication could not solve is _____

_____

H. We can learn to be more competent interpersonal communicators.

IV. Communication competence involves being both _____
and _____

A. Because no one style of communication works well in all situations, we must learn a variety of behaviors and know when each set of behaviors is most appropriate.

B. When individuals appropriately adapt their communication, they are sensitive to goals, contexts, and other people. An example of when I was sensitive to the needs of someone else and adapted my communication is _____

_____

C. By engaging in dual perspective, we can see not only our view of the interaction, but also the other person's view of self, the situation, and thoughts or feelings in an ethical manner. This involves considering the moral implications of what we say and do, as well as how this affects others.

D. Monitoring our communication involves observing and regulating how we communicate with others both before and during our interactions. One time I monitored my communication with others was _____

_____

E. We must be willing to commit the time and energy necessary to practice effective and ethical interpersonal communication in our relationships.

Additional Vocabulary

For each of the terms listed below, generate a personal example that illustrates the concept.

Communication competence _____

_____

Dual Perspective _____

_____

Ethics _____

_____

Metacommunication _____

_____

Monitoring _____

_____

Person-centered communication _____

_____

Symbols _____

_____

Key Concepts

content meaning
dual perspective
ethics
feedback
I-It communication
interactive models
interpersonal communication
interpersonal communication competence
I-Thou communication
I-You communication
linear models

metacommunication
models
monitoring
noise
person-centeredness
process
relationship meaning
symbols
systemic
transactional model

Activities

Title	Individual	Partner	Group	Ethno.	Internet/InfoTrac
1.1 Recognizing How Communication Meets Human Needs	✓				✓
1.2 Recognizing Needs That Motivate Communication	✓				
1.3 Observing Communication That Meets Needs	✓		✓		
1.4 Tuning In to Relational Level of Meaning	✓		✓		
1.5 Identifying Levels of Meaning in Your Communication	✓				
1.6 Assessing Satisfaction with Communication Skills	✓				
1.7 Understanding Communication Systems	✓				
1.8 Recognizing Dimensions of Relational Level Meanings	✓				
1.9 Interpersonal Communication Skills Training for Money	✓				✓

Name _____

Activity 1.1: Recognizing How Communication Meets Human Needs (Using the WWW)

Purpose: To increase awareness of how you use communication to meet your needs.

Instructions: For each of the six human needs discussed in the textbook and listed below, identify two recent experiences in which you used communication to meet this need. For more background information, visit this web site:
http://www.hcc.hawaii.edu/intranet/committees/FacDevCom/guidebk/teachtip/maslow.htm

Example

Physical needs: I made an appointment with my supervisor and suggested that our department institute 5-minute "stand and stretch" breaks each hour so my coworkers and I could reduce fatigue associated with our intense computer work.

Physical needs

1.

2.

Safety needs

1.

2.

Belonging (social) needs

1.

2.

Self-esteem needs

1.

2.

Self-actualization needs

1.

2.

Interacting with diverse people

1.

2.

Processing: Compare the experiences you listed with those of others in your class. Discuss the importance of the different needs in living a satisfying life. Do you think the needs are equally important or do you believe some are more important (central, necessary) than others?

Name _____

Activity 1.2: Recognizing Needs That Motivate Communication

Purpose: To increase awareness of how you use communication to meet your needs in interpersonal relationships.

Instructions: Identify a close friend or romantic partner with whom you will interact in the next week. Record the content of your communication in 10 interactions. For each recorded communication, identify the need that motivated the communication.

Description of Interaction	Need Motivating Communication
Example	
I asked Erika to go to a concert with me.	Belonging

1.

2.

3.

4.

5.

6.

7.

8.

9.

10.

Name _____

Activity 1.3: Observing Communication That Meets Needs

Purpose: To enhance your ability to notice the ways that others use communication to meet needs.

Instructions: Either individually or with others in your class, select an episode of a television program to watch. As you watch, use the chart below to classify each communication in terms of which human need it most clearly addresses.

Need	Number of times addressed
Physical needs	
Safety needs	
Belonging needs	
Self-esteem needs	
Self-actualization needs	

Processing

What can you conclude from your observations about the prevalence of communication that attempts to satisfy the five human needs?

If time allows, classify communication in a second television program of a different type. For instance, if you watched a prime-time situational comedy, classify communication in a daytime soap opera or a dramatic show. How does the prevalence of different needs vary with program types?

Name _____

Activity 1.4: Tuning In to the Relational Level of Meaning

<u>Purpose</u>: To increase awareness of the three dimensions relational level meanings in interpersonal communication.

<u>Instructions</u>: Read the dialogue below individually or with other members of your class. Identify relational levels of meaning that seem to be implied by each line of dialogue.

Jim: You haven't done the laundry this week.

Jan: Right, and you haven't done the shopping.

Jim: But laundry is more important than shopping. After all, we can't go anywhere without clothes.

Jan: We probably can't do much without food, either.

Jim: You're trying to divert the conversation away from laundry, which is the issue I brought up.

Jan: No. I am trying to make you aware that we both agreed to do certain chores around this place and you have been as bad as me about not getting to the chores you agreed to do.

Jim: Okay, fair enough. I see your point. I apologize for not doing the shopping. I'll do it tomorrow.

Jan: Thanks. I'll find time to do the laundry tonight so you won't have to shop in dirty clothes.

Jim: Good. I knew I could count on you.

Jan: Only if I can also count on you.

Name _____

Activity 1.5: Identifying Levels of Meaning in Your Communication

Purpose: To increase awareness of relational level meanings in your communication with others.

Instructions: Identify a close friend or romantic partner with whom you interact regularly and with whom you will spend time during the next week. Describe 5 interactions with that person. For each of the interactions, identify the content and relational levels of meaning in your verbal and nonverbal messages.

Interaction	Content Meaning	Relational Meaning
Example		
Called Lee to suggest we have lunch.	I am available for lunch.	I care about you.

1.

2.

3.

4.

5.

Name _____

Activity 1.6: Assessing Satisfaction with Communication Skills

Purpose: To allow you to assess how satisfied you are with your ability to communicate in different situations.

Instructions: Listed below are 10 communication situations. Imagine that you are involved in each situation. Then, indicate how confident you are that you could communicate competently using the following scale.

1. Very satisfied that I could communicate competently

2. Somewhat satisfied that I could communicate competently

3. Not sure how effectively I could communicate.

4. Somewhat dissatisfied with my ability to communicate effectively

5. Very dissatisfied with my ability to communicate effectively

_____ 1. Someone asks you personal questions that you feel uncomfortable answering. You'd like to tell the person that you don't want to answer, but you don't want to hurt the person's feelings.

_____ 2. You think a friend of yours is starting to drink more alcohol than is healthy. You want to bring up the topic with your friend, but you don't want to create a barrier in the friendship.

_____ 3. You really care about the person you've been dating recently, but neither of you has ever put your feelings in words. You'd like to express how you feel, but aren't sure how your partner will respond.

_____ 4. During a heated discussion about social issues, the person with whom you are talking says, "Why won't you hear me out fairly??!"

_____ 5. A friend shares his creative writing with you and asks if you think he has any talent. You don't think the writing is very good, and you need to respond to his request for an opinion.

_____ 6. Your roommate's habits are really getting on your nerves. You want to tell your roommate you're bothered, but you don't want to cause hurt.

_____ 7. A classmate asks you for notes for the classes he missed. You agree, but then discover he has missed nearly half of the classes and expects you to bail him out. You feel that's exploitive.

_____ 8. You go to a party and discover that you don't know anyone there.

_____ 9. The person you have been dating declares "I love you." You care about the person but your feelings are not love, at least not yet. The person expects some response from you.

_____ 10. A person that you care about comes to you whenever he has problems he wants to discuss, and you give him attention and advice. When you want to talk about your problems, however, he doesn't seem to have time. You want the friendship to continue, but you don't like feeling it's one-way.

_____ TOTAL (Add up the numbers you placed in each blank. Make sure that your total is between 10 and 50).

Processing

A score of 40 to 50 indicates that you are very satisfied with your ability to communicate in a range of interpersonal situations. A score of 25 to 39 indicates that you are either fairly satisfied with your ability to communicate in various situations or that you are highly satisfied with your communication skills in some situations and relatively dissatisfied with your skills in other situations. A score of 24 or lower indicates that you are less satisfied with your interpersonal communication skills than you would like to be.

If your score indicates you are moderately satisfied or dissatisfied with your interpersonal communication skills, notice whether your answers are extremes (1s and 5s) or tend to be more average. Extreme ratings indicate that you are very satisfied with your ability to interact in some situations and very dissatisfied with your ability to interact in others. You should focus on improving your skills in the specific situations that make you uneasy. If you have more average scores for most or all of the 10 items, then you might work on further enhancing skills that you already have.

Retake this questionnaire when you complete the course and compare your scores.

Name _____

Activity 1.7: Understanding Communication Systems

Purpose: To increase your understanding of the interrelatedness of parts of interpersonal communication.

Instructions

1.   Describe a major change that occurred in your life. Examples of major changes are coming to college, making a major romantic commitment, and experiencing a serious accident or illness.

2.   Describe specific ways in which the change affected you. Explain how it affected your feelings, your ability to do things, the people you interacted with, your priorities, and so forth.

3.   Identify 3 people who were close to you at the time the change occurred in your life. Describe how the change in your life affected each of them. Did you interact more or less with them? Did you alter the nature of your communication with them? Did your relationships with them change? Did you ask or expect new things of them?

4.   Reflect on the ways in which a change in one aspect of a communication system (in this case, the change you experienced) affects all other elements of a system (in this case, the 3 people who were close to you when the change occurred).

Describe the change in your life.

Describe specific ways in which the change affected your relationships, interaction patterns, and so forth.

Identify 3 people who were close to you at the time that the change in your life occurred. For each person, describe how the change affected your relationship and communication with that person.

Person 1:

Person 2:

Person 3:

Name _____

Activity 1.8: Recognizing Dimensions of Relational Level Meanings

Purpose: To increase your awareness of relational level meanings in interpersonal communication.

Instructions: Recall that relational level meanings have three dimensions: liking, responsiveness, and control. In each of the following examples of communication, identify which dimension of relational level meaning seems to predominate.

1.   When Frances's parents criticize her for not coming home more often from school, she responds by saying, "Look, I'm 20 years old and you can't expect me to be at home every weekend."

   Dimension of relational communication: _____

2.   Edwin says to his 5-year-old daughter, "You clean up your room right now."

   Dimension of relational communication: _____

3.   Adrienne asks her friend Malcolm if he wants to come over for dinner and conversation.

   Dimension of relational communication: _____

4.   Jerry tells his friend Michael about a personal problem, and Michael doesn't respond. Jerry then says, "Hey, am I invisible or something?"

   Dimension of relational communication: _____

5.   Alfonso says to his partner, "I think you are the greatest person in the world."

   Dimension of relational communication: _____

6. As Kim talks, Pat nods her head and smiles to show that she is following and interested in what Kim says.

    Dimension of relational communication: _____

Name _____

Activity 1.9: Interpersonal Communication Skills Training for Money (Using the WWW)

Purpose: To learn how interpersonal communication skills training is promoted on business web pages.

Instructions: Go to your favorite web search engine (such as Teoma, AltaVista, or Google) and search for business web sites devoted to "interpersonal communication training." Visit at least five web sites and determine how each web site markets its training courses or sessions on interpersonal communication. Record what each site claims participants will be able to do by enrolling in the course or training session. What similarities in interpersonal communication training can you identify across the different web sites? What differences can you identify? What communication theories, if any, are such organizations basing their training upon?

Web Site #1

Web Site #2

Web Site #3

Web Site #4

Web Site #5

Using Your Everyday Encounters Premium Website

Use your *Everyday Encounters* premium website for quick access to the electronic study resources that accompany this text. The *Everyday Encounters* web site offers an interactive version of many of the activities in this chapter. You can complete these activities online and submit them electronically to your instructor. All of the web links included in this chapter as well as in the accompanying main text chapter are maintained on the web site, accessible through http://www.thomsonedu.com.

Included on the website is access to the Continuing the Conversation video scenario and questions featured in this chapter. Watch, listen to, and analyze the Continuing the Conversation case featuring *The New Employee* included at the end of Chapter 1 in your main text. The full transcript of *The New Employee* conversation is included in your textbook. Watch, listen to, and critique the conversation by completing the Conversation Analysis. You can compare your response to the authors by clicking on the Submit button at the end of the form.

Websites of Interest

The following URLs are maintained and updated on the *Everyday Encounters* web site, accessible through http://www.thomsonedu.com. We recommend you begin your web searches at this site to ensure that the links listed below are still active.

Name: Four Principles of Interpersonal Communication
Developer: Donnell King
Brief Description: This webpage lists four principles of interpersonal communication that are necessary for everyday life functioning.
URL: http://www.pstcc.edu/facstaff/dking/interpr.htm

Name: The Y? Forum -- The National Forum on People's Differences
Developer: Phillip J. Milano
Brief Description: This site gives people an opportunity to ask people from different backgrounds questions they are not able to ask because of an inability to contact people from another culture or an uncomfortable feeling asking the questions.
URL: http://www.yforum.com/

Name: Maslow's Hierarchy of Needs
Developer: Source Unknown; Honolulu Community College's web site
Brief Description: This page summarizes Abraham Maslow's hierarchy of needs.
http://www.hcc.hawaii.edu/intranet/committees/FacDevCom/guidebk/teachtip/maslow.htm

Name: World Hello Day

Developer: Jon H. Larsen and the World Hello Day Organization

Brief Description: This site provides the history for "World Hello Day" which is an annual event where people are asked to greet ten others as way of demonstrating the importance of personal communication for preserving peace.

URL: http://www.worldhelloday.org/

Name: Conversation as Communication

Developer: Gerard M. Blair

Brief Description: This web page offers an article that views communication as a process of simple planning and control. Students can contrast this view with the definition of communication in the text. The article discusses practical applications of this model of communication in the context of business meetings.

URL: http://www.ee.ed.ac.uk/~gerard/Management/art7.html

Name: Information Age: People, Information & Technology

Developer: Smithsonian Institution

Brief Description: This page contains "photographs from the exhibition, Information Age: People, Information & Technology in the Smithsonian's National Museum of American History. The exhibition displays visually and interactively how electrical information technology has changed our society over the last 150 years."

URL: http://photo2.si.edu/infoage/infoage.html

Name: Face to Face Communication Skills Library

Developer: Management Assistance Programs for Nonprofits; Carter McNamara

Brief Description: This site provides a library of resources for not-for-profit and for-profit businesses on a range of issues, including face to face communication.

URL: http://www.managementhelp.org/commskls/cmm_face.htm

Name: Do You Get Your Messages Across? Interpersonal Communication Skills Test

Developer: Queendom.com

Brief Description: This site provides an online test to evaluate general levels of communication skills.

URL: http://www.queendom.com/tests/relationships/communication_skills_r_access.html

Name: Benton Foundation's Best Practices Toolkit

Developer: Benton Foundation

Brief Description: This site is a Best Practices Toolkit of "Strategic Communications" from the Benton Foundation. The resources are supposed to help nonprofit organizations use communications technologies effectively in support of their missions.

URL: http://www.benton.org/publibrary/toolkits/stratcommtool.html

Name: Ethics, Leadership, and Communication Issue-Portal

Developer: Ivy Sea Online

Brief Description: Part of a series of Ivy Sea's hot-issue portals, this portal focuses on ethics in business and addresses topics such as the high cost of incivility and miscommunication.
URL: http://www.ivysea.com/pages/ethicsportal.html

Name: Interpersonal Communication Tops Concerns of Farm Supervisors
Developer: Gregorio Billikopf Encina, University of California, Berkeley
Brief Description: This webpage reports on a study Encina conducted with 42 farm supervisors in the northern San Joaquin Valley. Of no surprise to students of interpersonal communication, developing productive personal relationships was central to supervisors' success.
URL:http://www.cnr.berkeley.edu/ucce50/ag-labor/7research/7calag10.htm

Self Test

Multiple Choice

_____ 1. Which of the following is not a physical need?

    A. the need to breathe
    B. the need to eat
    C. the need for water or other beverages
    D. the need for safe shelter

_____ 2. Transactional models of communication emphasize the simultaneous nature of transactions in which the communicator is

    A. the sender
    B. the receiver
    C. not affected by noise
    D. both sender and receiver

_____ 3. Monitoring is best defined as:

    A. the ability to engage in dual perspective.
    B. the ability to observe and regulate oneself.
    C. the ability to interpret relational meanings.
    D. development of a range of communication skills.

_____ 4. For ethical communication to occur, you must:

    A. communicate whatever is on their minds.
    B. commit to honor others and yourself.
    C. attend to others' needs rather than their own needs.
    D. agree that one person will always have more power in the relationship than the other person.

_____ 5. The primary contribution modification that interactive models of communication offered to the existing model was:

    A. feedback.
    B. noise.
    C. different channels of communication.
    D. the recognition of communication as a one-way process.

_____ 6. An example of metacommunication is

A. "Will you please take out the trash?"
B. "That's a colorful sweater."
C. "Did you try the shrimp? It's very spicy."
D. "When might we talk about us?"

True/False

____ 7. Communication is an ongoing, systemic process which simultaneously occurs in three dimensions.

____ 8. I-You communication is the most frequent kind of communication.

____ 9. Content-level meanings express the relationship between communicators.

____ 10. All cultures and societies think it's useful to communicate extensively about feelings.

____ 11. Words have inherent, or true meanings, despite the fact that they are simple symbols.

____ 12. Relational-level meanings express liking, responsiveness, and power between communicators.

Essay

14. Choose four of the eight basic principles for effective interpersonal communication. For each principle, provide an example of how that principle applies to you.

15. Name and give a personal example of how you use communication to fulfill each of the five basic needs.

Personal Reflections

1. Describe an I–It, I–You, and I–Thou relationship in your life (one each). Analyze differences in communication and personal knowledge in the three relationships.
2. Describe and analyze two communication rules in your family of origin. Trace how they affected patterns of interaction among family members.
3. Because interpersonal communication affects us and others, our interactions involve ethical choices. Describe a situation that involved an ethical choice and the communication practices used to address the issue.

Chapter 2: Communication and the Creation of Self

I.   The self is a complicated, multidimensional process.

      A.   We develop notions of who we are and aren't because of our interactions with others from the time we are born until the time we die.

            1.   We develop images of ourselves, both positive and negative, based upon the messages others communicate to us.

                  a.   An example of a positive <u>self-fulfilling prophecy</u> is

_____

_____

_____

                  b.   An example of a negative <u>self-fulfilling prophecy</u> is

_____

_____

_____

            2.   Communication with three different groups of people is most influential in helping us develop our self.

                  a.   Family members are usually the first to influence our development of the self.

                        i.   Family members provide <u>direct definitions</u> by labeling our behaviors and us. An example of a direct definition my family provided for me is _____

_____

ii.   Family members also provide <u>identity scripts</u> that define our roles, how we play them, and the general progression of our life. An example of an identity script in my family is _____

_____

iii.   Parents or primary care givers communicate who we are by how they interact with us, or their <u>attachment styles</u>. In my family, we had a(n) _____ attachment style because we interacted with each other by _____

_____

b.   Early in life we begin to interact with our peers who also help us figure out who we are.

i.   <u>Reflected appraisals</u> indicate who our peers believe us to be as well as what behaviors are appropriate or inappropriate in these interactions. An example of a reflected appraisal from my life is

_____

ii.   We also compare ourselves with those around us. An example of a <u>social comparison</u> in which I engaged recently is _____

_____

c.   Society as a whole also influences how we see our behavior and ourselves.

i.   The <u>generalized other</u> reflects the views that others in a society generally hold.

        ii.   Perspectives of the generalized other are communicated through the media, institutions, and individuals who have internalized or reflect cultural values.

B.   There are many different ways we view our selves, including physical, emotional, social, and moral.

C.   Because it involves a process, the self develops over the course of time.

    1.   Ego boundaries define where an individual stops and the world begins.

    2.   Development of the self is a continuous process.

D.   Two kinds of social perspectives help us define our self because we learn what society values and generally develop a shared sense of what is important to thrive.

    1.   <u>Particular others</u> are specific individuals, who we consider significant in our lives, that show how they see us. Particular others in my life include _____

    _____

    2.   The <u>generalized other</u> is a collection of rules, roles, and attitudes accepted as appropriate by the social community in which we live.

        a.   Race, gender, sexual orientation, and socioeconomic class are prevalent identifiers in Western culture.

        b.   The generalized other unequally values different races, genders, socioeconomic classes, and sexual orientations.

E.   Because social perspectives are defined in a particular time and place, they are open to revision as our situations change.

II.   There are four guidelines for strengthening our self or view or our identity.

A.   We must make a commitment to finding ways to help us grow. An example of a way that I can help myself grow is _____

_____

B.   Once we are committed, it is important to understand how our self has developed as well as what changes are desirable and how to help them happen. An example of a change I would like to make is _____

_____

I can aid in the process by _____

_____

C.   Rather than setting ourselves up for failure by attempting to make radical changes in our self, we need to set realistic goals with realistic standards.

D.   We need to choose settings that and people who will help us achieve our goals.

    1.   *Uppers* are people who communicate positively about us and reflect positive appraisals of our value as individuals. Someone who can serve as an upper in helping me achieve my goal is _____

_____

    2.   *Downers* are people who communicate negatively about us and reflect negative appraisals of our value as individuals. Someone who would keep me from achieving my goal is _____

_____

    3.   *Vultures* are extreme versions of downers. They communicate negatively about us by attacking our view of self. Someone who would sabotage my attempt to

reach my goal is _____

_____

4.   *Self-sabotage* occurs when we act as a downer or vulture for ourselves. One way

I am going to avoid self-sabotage is _____

_____

Additional Vocabulary

For each of the terms listed below, generate a personal example that illustrates the concept.

Ego boundaries _____

_____

Generalized other _____

_____

Identity scripts _____

_____

Key Concepts

anxious-ambivalent attachment style
attachment styles
direct definition
dismissive attachment style
downers
ego boundaries
fearful attachment style
generalized other
identity scripts
Johari window

particular others
reflected appraisal
secure attachment style
self
self-disclosure
self-fulfilling prophecy
self-sabotage
social comparison
uppers
vultures

Activities

Title	Individual	Partner	Group	Ethno.	Internet/InfoTrac
2.1 Recognizing the Communication of Uppers, Downers, & Vultures	✓	✓	✓	✓	✓
2.2 Comparing Your Views and Others' Views of Yourself	✓	✓	✓	✓	✓
2.3 Tracing Changes in Social Perspectives	✓	✓	✓	✓	✓
2.4 Recognizing Your Social Comparisons	✓	✓	✓	✓	✓
2.5 Identifying Your Identity Scripts	✓	✓	✓	✓	✓
2.6 Cultural Variations in Social Perspectives	✓	✓	✓	✓	✓
2.7 Improving Self Concept	✓	✓	✓	✓	✓
2.8 My Personal Web Page	✓	✓	✓	✓	✓
2.9 Your Many Windows	✓	✓	✓	✓	✓

Name _____

Activity 2.1: Recognizing the Communication of Uppers, Downers, & Vultures

<u>Purpose</u>: To increase your awareness of the communication styles of people who are uppers, downers, and vultures.

<u>Instructions</u>: Identify three people with whom you interact. One person should be someone who is an upper for you; the second person should be a downer for you; the third person should be a vulture for you. Write the names of the three people in the three blanks at the left of the form below. Beside each name, describe specific verbal and nonverbal communication that the person uses to enact the role of upper, downer, or vulture.

Role/Person	Verbal Communication	Nonverbal Communication
Example		
Upper/ Louise	Compliments me. Talks about strengths.	Smiles when she sees me. Looks interested when I am talking to her.

Upper/ _____

Downer/_____

Vulture/_____

Name _____

Activity 2.2: Comparing Your Views and Others' Views of Yourself

Purpose: To provide insight into how you and others perceive you, and differences in the two views of you.

Instructions:

Fill out the form below by indicating how true of you think each statement is.

Ask someone you think knows you well to fill out the duplicate form that follows. Write your name in the blank spaces on the second form.

Compare the two views of you. Discuss differences with the other person and try to understand why you and the other person might perceive you differently.

Rate each item for how true it is of you. Use the following scale:

1 = very true or always true

2 = mostly true or usually true

3 = somewhat true or true in some situations

4 = mostly untrue or usually untrue

5 = untrue or never true

_____ 1. I am an optimistic person.

_____ 2. I am personally mature.

_____ 3. I am extroverted.

_____ 4. I am thoughtful about others and their feelings.

_____ 5. I am ambitious.

_____ 6. I am generally cheerful, or upbeat.

_____ 7. I am moody.

_____ 8. I am a reliable friend.

_____ 9. I am unconventional in my beliefs.

_____ 10. I am assertive.

Form to be filled out by person who knows you well

Rate each item for how true it is of _____. Use the following scale:

1 = very true or always true

2 = mostly true or usually true

3 = somewhat true or true in some situations

4 = mostly untrue or usually untrue

5 = untrue or never true

_____   1.   _____ is an optimistic person.

_____   2.   _____ is personally mature.

_____   3.   _____ is extroverted.

_____   4.   _____ is thoughtful about others and their feelings.

_____   5.   _____ is ambitious.

_____   6.   _____ is cheerful, or upbeat.

_____   7.   _____ is moody.

_____   8.   _____ is a reliable friend.

_____   9.   _____ is unconventional in his/her beliefs.

_____   10.   _____ is assertive.

Name _____

Activity 2.3: Tracing Changes in Social Perspectives

Purpose: To increase awareness of how social perspectives change over time within a single society.

Instructions:

1.   Identify a person (a family member, acquaintance, or friend) who is 10 to 15 years older than you. Identify another person who is 25 or more years older than you. Identify a third person who is 10 to 15 years younger than you.

2.   Write your views of women and men—what they should be like and do; what is unfeminine and unmasculine.

3.   Ask each of the three persons you identified to describe his or her views of women and men. Ask them what women should be like and what men should be like. Encourage them to explain what they consider to be unfeminine and unmasculine behaviors, attitudes, roles, and so forth.

4.   Compare the views of people of different ages, including yourself as one of the people.

Discuss your findings with others in your class to discover whether there are trends in the views of gender that are common in groups of different ages.

Views of gender of person 10-15 years younger than me.

My views of gender.

Views of gender of person 10-15 years older than me.

Views of gender of person 25+ years older than me.

Name _____

Activity 2.4: Recognizing Your Social Comparisons

<u>Purpose</u>: To enhance awareness of the influence of social comparisons on your self-concept.

<u>Instructions</u>:

1.   List 3 positive qualities or abilities of yours and 3 negative qualities or areas in which you think you are unskillful. Write these in the left column of the chart.

2.   Identify two people you consider particularly skilled in each of the 6 areas. Identify how you compare to those two specific people.

3.   Substitute two different people as comparison points for each quality. Consider how using the substitutes as comparison points alters your view of your own strengths and weaknesses.

Reflect on how the skill of the people you select as points for social comparison affect your views of yourself.

With others in your class, discuss the importance of realistic choices of people to be our points of social comparison.

Positive Qualities/

Areas of Skill	Person 1	Person 2
1.		
2.		
3.		

Negative Qualities/

Areas of Lack of Skill	Person 1	Person 2
1.		
2.		
3.		

Positive Qualities/

Areas of Skill	Substitute Person 1	Substitute Person 2
1.		
2.		
3.		

Negative Qualities/

Areas of Lack of Skill	Substitute Person 1	Substitute Person 2
1.		
2.		
3.		

Activity 2.5: Identifying Your Identity Scripts

Purpose: To help you recognize identity scripts communicated to you by members of your family.

Instructions:

Complete each sentence below by filling in what members of your family told you when you were a young child. Put a check by each of the scripts that you still act on.

Assess how these scripts enhance and/or interfere with your life today and your current goals.

Money is

Nobody in our family has ever

You can/cannot (circle one) trust others.

The most important goal in life is

Good people

You can't trust people who

Families should

If you want others to respect you, you should

Name _____

Activity 2.6: Cultural Variations in Social Perspectives
(Using the WWW)

Purpose: To increase awareness of cultural differences in social views.

Instructions

1.   Write your definitions of the terms on the form below. Explain whether you have positive or negative views of each term and how important each term is to your view of yourself.

2.   Select two individuals with ethnic heritages that differ from yours. Ask each of them to define the terms on the form below. You can visit the web site http://www.yforum.com/ in order to ask questions of a person from a cultural background different from yours.

3.   Compare views among different cultures.

Term	Your View	Person A's View	Person B's View
Family			
Individual			
Assertion			

Term	Your View	Person A's View	Person B's View
Competition			
Nature			
Divorce			
Modesty			
Honor			

Name _____

Activity 2.7: Improving Self Concept

Purpose: To guide you through the process of initiating changes in yourself.

Instructions: Identify one aspect of your interpersonal communication that you would like to change. Keeping that aspect in mind, apply the guidelines below to help you succeed in bringing about the change that you desire. Since changing the self is a process, don't expect immediate results. Instead, keep the form below with you and refer back to it at regular intervals during the academic term. Make notes on progress you make in achieving the change you desire.

Identify an aspect of your interpersonal communication that you wish to change (examples: I want to be a better listener; I want to be less judgmental; I want to be more assertive):

Identify potential barriers to change (example: many of my friends are judgmental and this reinforces my own tendency to be judgmental):

Identify sources of knowledge that might help you achieve the change you desire (examples: I could check the library for books on judgmental attitudes and see what the experts say about changing this; I could observe Shelley closely since I think she is very nonjudgmental):

Set realistic goals (example: I am not trying to erase judgment from my attitudes; I only want to lessen its pervasiveness in my thinking.

Assess yourself fairly (example: I don't have to be as non-judgmental as Shelley; I could also compare myself to Marilyn who is even more judgmental than I am now):

Create a supportive context for change (examples: I will spend more time with Shelley; I will resist engaging in self-sabotage with negative self-talk):

Accept yourself as in process, and realize that change is more likely to be gradual and incremental than abrupt and complete.

Assessment of yourself today:

Assessment of yourself in 2 weeks:

Assessment of yourself in 1 month:

Assessment of yourself in 2 months:

Assessment of yourself at the end of the term:

Name _____

Activity 2.8: My Personal Web Page
(Using the WWW)

Purpose: To learn about the type of information that is include and excluded from personal home pages.

Instructions: Visit five personal web pages (you can search for people's personal home pages at a number of community sites, such as http://www.aol.com/community/directory.html; click on "Find Home Pages"). Make a list of the type of information, graphics, pictures, etc. each person puts on their home page and then count how many times each kind of information appears on the home pages. What kind of information appeared the most? What type of information was not included? Do you notice any other patterns, such as gender differences, in terms of what type of information is displayed?

Web Site #1:

Web Site #2:

Web Site #3:

Web Site #4:

Web Site #5:

Name _____

Activity 2.9: Your Many Windows

Purposes: To allow you to apply the Johari Window to your life to discover content in the different windows of yourself; To increase awareness of differences in what is communicated about the self in different relationships.

Instructions

1. If you do not recall the textbook's discussion of the Johari Window, review *Guidelines for Improving Self-Concept* before proceeding with this activity.

2. On the following pages you will find three copies of blank Johari Windows--one each for your parent, your best friend, and a past or current romantic partner. Fill in each Johari Window by writing information about you that fits each pane in the window for that particular relationship.

3. When you have filled in all three Johari Windows, compare the kinds of information that fits in each pane among the different relationships.

Relationship 1: With a parent (either parent)

	Known to Self	Unknown to Self
k **n** **o** **w** **n** **t** **o** **o** **t** **h** **e** **r** **s**	Open Area	Blind Area
u **n** **k** **n** **o** **w** **n** **t** **o** **o** **t** **h** **e** **r** **s**	Hidden Area	Unknown Area

Relationship 2: With your best friend

	Known to Self	Unknown to Self
k n o w n t o o t h e r s	Open Area	Blind Area
u n k n o w n t o o t h e r s	Hidden Area	Unknown Area

56

Relationship 3: With a current or former romantic partner

	Known to Self	Unknown to Self
known to others	Open Area	Blind Area
unknown to others	Hidden Area	Unknown Area

Using Your *Everyday Encounters* Premium Website

Use your *Everyday Encounters* premium website for quick access to the electronic study resources that accompany this text. The *Everyday Encounters* web site offers an interactive version of many of the activities in this chapter. You can complete these activities online and submit them electronically to your instructor. All of the web links included in this chapter as well as in the accompanying main text chapter are maintained on the web site, accessible through http://www.thomsonedu.com.

Included on the website is access to the Continuing the Conversation video scenario and questions featured in this chapter. Watch, listen to, and analyze the Continuing the Conversation case featuring *Does He Treat You Right?* which is included at the end of Chapter 2 in your main text. The full transcript of *Does He Treat You Right?* conversation is included in your textbook. Watch, listen to and critique the conversation by completing the Conversation Analysis. You can compare your response to the authors by clicking on the Submit button at the end of the form.

Websites of Interest

The following URLs are maintained and updated on the *Everyday Encounters* web site, accessible through http://www.thomsonedu.com. We recommend you begin your web searches at this site to ensure that the links listed below are still active.

Name: Joining the Size Acceptance Revolution
Developer: National Association to Advance Fat Acceptance
Brief Description: This web-based brochure talks about U.S. culture's idealization of slenderness and how this affects the self-concepts of those who are larger than average.
URL: http://www.naafa.org/documents/brochures/revolution.html

Name: The Curse of the Self
Developers: Mark Leary; Wake Forest University
Brief Description: From Mark Leary's book by the same name, this web page explores the personal difficulties created by one's self-reflection and offers tips on minimizing those difficulties.
URL: http://www.curseoftheself.com

Name: Self
Developer: Living Life Fully
Brief Description: This page lists quotations about the self from a variety of sources.
URL: http://www.livinglifefully.com/self.html

Name: Communication and Identity in Cyberspace
Developer: Dr. Daniel Chandler, University of Wales at Aberystwyth

Brief Description: This web page is a workshop-based module and is designed to help students raise awareness of issues of communication and identity on the Internet.
URL: http://www.aber.ac.uk/media/Modules/MC30920/homepage.html

Name: Name Changes
Developer: About.com
Brief Description: This web page offers various options for women regarding name changes when they marry. It also includes an interactive poll with statistics about which choices people have made.
URL: http://careerplanning.about.com/od/forwomenonly/a/name_change.htm

Name: Johari Window Questionnaire
Developer: Lyn Colangelo; Austin Community College
Brief Description: The questionnaire is designed to identify the different aspects of an individual's own Johari Window.
URL: http://www.austincc.edu/colangelo/1311/johari.htm

Self Test

Multiple Choice

_____ 1. Andrea says to her daughter, Bethany, "You really stand up for yourself!" This is an example of:

    A. reflected appraisal.
    B. self-sabotage.
    C. direct definition.
    D. attachment style.

_____ 2. Research has found that individuals with a(n) _____ attachment style often develop a view of relationships as being unnecessary or undesirable.

    A. secure
    B. fearful
    C. dismissive
    D. anxious/ambivalent

_____ 3. Cedric says, "Daddy says I am strong, so I must be strong." The son's comment illustrates

    A. reflected appraisal
    B. identity script
    C. ego boundaries
    D. social comparison

_____ 4. Chuck plays ball with his friends and realizes that two of them are better catchers than he is. Chuck thinks, "I am not as good a catcher as I thought." Chuck's reassessment of his catching ability is prompted by

    A. social comparison
    B. direct definition
    C. self-sabotage
    D. reflected appraisal

_____ 5. The development of the self begins with:

    A. our views of who we are.
    B. others' views of who we are.
    C. our views of who others are.
    D. others' views of who they are.

_____ 6. The general views and values endorsed by a society or social group are called:

    A. the perspective of particular others.
    B. self-fulfilling prophecy.
    C. the perspective of the generalized other.
    D. identity scripts.

_____ 7. Brenda says to her brother, "I know you're not happy with your performance at the last swim meet. However, with a little work on your kicking style, you'll be unstoppable." Brenda's statement to her brother is an example of:

    A. being a vulture.
    B. engaging in self-sabotage.
    C. being a downer.
    D. being an upper.

True/False

_____ 8. As babies, we develop a self-concept as soon as we can look within ourselves.

_____ 9. Self-disclosure is an important way for us to learn about ourselves.

_____ 10. Improving the self-concept is not challenging—it just requires thoughtful planning.

_____ 11. "Ego boundaries" is defined as the deliberate revealing of information about ourselves.

_____ 12. The perspectives that impact us the most, beginning at birth, are those of generalized others.

Essay

13. Describe one change you would like to make in yourself. Relying on the discussion in Chapter 2 of your text, explain how you could create a context that supports the change you wish to make. What obstacles might you encounter?

14. Identify the ways in which social categories emphasized by the generalized other in the U.S., including gender, race, sexual orientation, and socioeconomic class, intersect in your own view of self (e.g., female, African-American, bisexual, upper-middle class; or male, Latino, heterosexual, middle-class). How do the perspectives of the generalized other influence your view of self?

15. Identify the four attachment styles and use examples to illustrate each one. How has each attachment style influenced relationships?

Personal Reflections

1. Read through a commercial magazine and identify examples of the Generalized Other's perspective. Focus on how media define desirable women and men. Analyze these messages and discuss how you respond to them.

2. Describe an instance in which you were each of the following: an Upper, a Downer, and a Vulture. Analyze why you communicated differently in the different situations. What was it about the overall communication systems that affected what you said, and how did your communication, in turn, affect the relational systems within which it occurred?

3. Identify three different contexts in which you regularly communicate (e.g., school, family, friends). Next, describe how you view yourself in each context. What similarities can you recognize across the three contexts in your view of self? What differences exist? Why do you think those differences/similarities occur?

Chapter 3:   Perception and Communication

I.   Perception is an active process of creating meaning by selecting, organizing, and interpreting people, objects, events, situation, and activities. Essentially, how do we make sense of what happens in the world around us?

     A.   We consciously select which of the infinite number of stimuli around us is most relevant at any point in time. Stop what you are doing for a moment and write down one example of something you see: _____;
something you smell: _____;
something you hear: _____;
something you feel: _____;
and something going on inside your body: _____.

         1.   We select stimuli that stand out above the others. _____
_____ is the stimulus that stood out most in my list above.

         2.   We influence what we select by noticing things we had not noticed before. In class today, one thing I noticed that I had not noticed before was _____.

         3.   Who we are, what we need, why we need it, and where we are at a moment in time influences what we select. In class, I am most tuned in to
_____
because _____.

         4.   The culture in which we grow up and live also influences what we select to perceive. Because I grew up in _____,
I am more likely to notice _____
_____.

B. We use four organizational structures (schemata) to make sense of what we have selected to notice.

    1. Prototypes represent the most typical or ideal example of a particular group of people, places, objects, activities, relationships, or events. A <u>prototype</u> for

       _____ is

       _____

    2. Personal constructs are bipolar dimensions of judgment we use to determine where someone or something fits. When I meet someone new, the <u>personal constructs</u> I use to judge that person are _____

    3. Stereotypes are generalizations that we perceive represent a majority, but not all, of the people or things in a particular category. Stereotypes allow us to create a set of expected behaviors. An example of a <u>stereotype</u> that I have for

       _____ is

       _____

    4. Scripts are a sequence of behaviors that we have for how we and others should act in particular situations. An example of a <u>script</u> we use in my family is _____

       _____

C. Interpretation is the process of attaching meaning or explanations to what we have noticed and organized.

    1. Attributions are explanations for why things happen or people act the way they do. An example of an <u>attribution</u> I made yesterday was _____

       _____

       _____

2. Attribution errors occur when we attach distorted meanings to what happens around us.

    a. A self-serving bias occurs when we take excessive personal credit for our successes or assume someone or something else is responsible for our poor performances. An example of a time when I committed the <u>self serving bias</u> is _____

       _____

    b. A fundamental attribution error occurs when we overestimate the internal causes and underestimate the external causes of others' undesirable behaviors or when we overestimate the external causes and underestimate the internal causes of our undesirable behaviors. An example of a time when I committed the <u>fundamental attribution error</u> is

       _____

II. At least six factors affect our perception process.

    A. Human physiology indicates that not everyone's five senses, biorhythms, or medical conditions are exactly the same. An example of how human physiology affected my perception today was _____

       _____

    B. Age and the number of experiences accompanying it alter our view or interpretation of particular communication situations. One of the things that I perceive differently than people in the generation before me is _____

       _____

C.   Our culture leads each of us to have a particular set of beliefs, values, understandings, practices that influence our perception process. Because of my <u>culture</u>, today I perceived _____ differently than someone in another culture would.

D.   Our various <u>standpoints</u>, or social groups to which we belong in a particular culture, shape our point of view. An example of a time my _____ standpoint shaped how I perceived a person or situation was _____

       _____   _____   _____

E.   How we are taught to enact social roles, and the behaviors we actually perform to carry out our social roles, influence how we perceive the world around us. An example of a time when my social role influenced my perception of a person or behavior is _____

       _____

F.   Cognitive abilities indicate the number of different interpretations we can create for a situation.

       1.   People who have more schemata for organizing and interpreting situations are considered more cognitively complex.

       2.   When using person-centered communication we interact with an individual as a unique human being. An example of a time when I used <u>person-centered communication</u> is _____

              _____

       3.   We empathize with another when we do our best to feel what another person is feeling in a particular situation. A recent experience in which I used empathy is

              _____

G.   Our selves also influence how we select, organize, and interpret stimuli.

1.   Attachment styles influence how we perceive others, situations, and messages. An example of when my attachment style influenced how I perceived someone else is_____

_____ .

2.   We have implicit personality theories of interaction characteristics that we believe go together. An example of a time when I used the implicit personality theory is_____

_____

III.   There are many ways we can improve the accuracy of our perceptions.

A.   We need to understand that all of our perceptions occur at a point in time, represent only a portion of the stimuli we could notice, and cannot be determined to be true or false. An example of a time when I should have noticed that perceptions are static, partial, and unverifiable is _____

_____

B.   We need to avoid assuming that we know what another person thinks or how she or he perceives a particular situation. An example of a time when I should have avoided assuming is _____

_____

C.   Perception checking occurs when we ask others to check the extent to which our perceptions are accurate so that we can create a shared understanding of each other, the situation, and our relationship. An example of a time when I should have engaged in perception checking is _____

_____

D.   We need to recognize the difference between facts (those things we can verify based on observation) and inferences (those things we create by interpreting what we have observed). An example of a time when I should not have confused facts and inferences is

_____.

E.   We need to guard against self serving bias because it can distort our perceptions. One time when the self serving bias distorted my perceptions is _____

_____.

F.   We can avoid the fundamental attribution error by looking for external reasons for others' actions and internal motivations for our own. An example of a time when I should have guarded against the fundamental attribution error is _____

_____.

G.   We need to remember that the label we attach to a particular interaction affects not only how we perceive that situation, but also how we will behave in future interactions. An example of a time when I should have paid more attention to labels is _____

_____.

Additional Vocabulary

For each of the terms listed below, generate a personal example that illustrates the concept.

Cognitive Complexity _____

_____

Mindreading _____

_____

Key Concepts

attributions

cognitive complexity

constructivism

culture

empathy

fundamental attribution error

implicit personality theory

interpretation

mindreading

perception

personal constructs

prototypes

scripts

self-serving bias

standpoint theory

stereotypes

Activities

Title	Individual	Partner	Group	Ethno.	Internet/InfoTrac
3.1 Observing the Impact of Language on Perceptions	✓			✓	✓
3.2 Distinguishing Facts from Inferences	✓		✓		
3.3 Remaking the Social World			✓		
3.4 Instructor Perceptions	✓				
3.5 Categorizing Race and Ethnicity	✓				✓

Name _____

Activity 3.1: Observing the Impact of Language on Perceptions (With InfoTrac-College Edition)

<u>Purpose</u>: To increase awareness of the influence of language on human perception.

<u>Instructions</u>

Ask 5 people the questions 1 and 2 in the form below and record their answers.

Ask 5 different people questions 3 and 4 in the form below and record their answers.

1.   Did you see the article on tuition increases in today's campus newspaper?

Answer 1:

Answer 2:

Answer 3:

Answer 4:

Answer 5:

2.   How much do you think this school can inflate the cost of tuition?

Answer 1:

Answer 2:

Answer 3:

Answer 4:

Answer 5:

3.   Did you see an article on tuition increases in today's campus newspaper?

Answer 1:

Answer 2:

Answer 3:

Answer 4:

Answer 5:

4.   How much do you think this school can nudge the cost of tuition.

Answer 1:

Answer 2:

Answer 3:

Answer 4:

Answer 5:

Compare and contrast the answers you got for the definite questions with the answers you got for the indefinite questions.

Visit *InfoTrac-College Edition* and search for articles with the keywords "language and perception*" (perception* asks InfoTrac to search for articles with the keywords "perception" and "perceptions"). Skim the article entitled "Technical Language, Advice Understandability, and Perceptions of Expertise and Trustworthiness: The Case of the Financial Planner" and discuss selected points in class.

Name _____

Activity 3.2: Distinguishing Facts from Inferences

<u>Purpose</u>: To increase your skill in distinguishing between facts and inferences.

<u>Instructions</u>: Read the story below. Then decide whether each of the statements that follow the story is a fact or an inference.

Chris went to the mall to get a new compact disc. Even though Chris didn't have the money to pay for it, Chris really wanted the CD. After looking in several stores and comparing prices, Chris found the least expensive CD, but it still cost $30. Chris knew it was not affordable. Later when Chris was playing a new CD for friends, they all complimented Chris on such great taste in music.

1.   Chris bought the $30 compact disc.

2.   Chris stole the $30 compact disc.

3.   Chris left the mall with the $30 compact disc.

4.   Chris really wanted the new compact disc.

5.   Chris is irresponsible with money.

Do you believe Chris is male or female? Why?

Only statement four is factual. The others are inferences that go beyond the facts presented in the story. We know only that Chris went to the mall to get a compact disc and later Chris played a new compact disc. We do not know WHICH compact disc Chris played and we do not know whether Chris charged them on credit, paid in cash, or shoplifted the compact disc. We also don't have facts that would allow us to determine whether Chris is irresponsible with money.

If you made mistakes, why do you think you made them? If you got all of them correct, what kept you from making mistakes?

Name _____

Activity 3.3: Remaking the Social World

Purposes: To enhance your awareness of the arbitrariness and the impact of categories that societies use to define people; and to allow you to imagine how society would be different if different categories for defining people were used.

Instructions: Join with 5 or 6 other people in your class to form a discussion group. Your group's task is to devise a method of classifying people and to suggest some of the implications of the classifications that you devise. The only restriction on how you complete the task is that you may not use race, class, sex, or sexual orientation to define and classify individuals.

After 20 minutes of group discussion, make a report to the class in which you:

   A.   Describe your system of classifying people.

   B.   Provide a rationale for the method of classification you chose.

   C.   Explain some of the political, economic, educational, and social consequences that would
         be likely if people were classified and, thus perceived, only with reference to your
         system.

Name _____

Activity 3.4: Instructor Perceptions

<u>Purpose</u>: To examine some of the perception mistakes we can make; and to test the guidelines for making more accurate perceptions.

<u>Instructions</u>: Complete each of the questions listed below for an instructor other than the one who teaches your interpersonal communication class.

1.   Write down what you remember about your instructor on the first day of class (e.g., what she or he was wearing; what did that person tell you about himself or herself).

2.   What kind of car do you think this person drives? Why?

3.   Where do you think this person grew up? Why?

4.   What do you think this person does when she or he is not working (at school teaching or at home preparing for class, grading papers, or conducting research)? Why?

5.   How do you think this person grades? Why?

6.   Would this person get along with your friends? Why or why not?

7.   What three adjectives would you use to describe this person? Why?

If you feel comfortable approaching this instructor, ask him or her how she or he would have answered the above questions. Based upon what you know about improving perception, what could you have done differently to avoid the misperceptions you made? Why do you think you got the answers right that you did?

If you do not feel comfortable approaching this instructor, what could you have done to make sure your perceptions were more accurate?

Name _____

Activity 3.5: Categorizing Race and Ethnicity
(Using the WWW)

Categorizing Race and Ethnicity

<u>Purpose</u>: To learn how race and ethnicity is organized into categories and whether or not they are sufficient to account for individual's sense of racial and ethnic identity.

<u>Instructions</u>: In the left column, describe your ethnic and racial background. In the right column, make a list of the current categories the U.S. Census Bureau used in the 2000 U.S. Census (to find out this information, go to the U.S. Census Bureau's web site at http://www.census.gov/population/www/socdemo/race/racefactcb.html). Which box would you check on the census form? Do you feel the U.S. Census Bureau's category are an accurate representation of the diversity of ethnic backgrounds in the U.S.?

My Ethnic and Racial Background   **U.S. Census Bureau Categories**

Using Your Everyday Encounters Premium Website

Use your *Everyday Encounters* premium website for quick access to the electronic study resources that accompany this text. The *Everyday Encounters* web site offers an interactive version of many of the activities in this chapter. You can complete these activities online and submit them electronically to your instructor. All of the web links included in this chapter as well as in the accompanying main text chapter are maintained on the web site, accessible through http://www.thomsonedu.com.

Included on the website is access to the Continuing the Conversation video scenario and questions featured in this chapter. Watch, listen to, and analyze the Continuing the Conversation case featuring *College Success: Two Perspectives* included at the end of Chapter 3 in your main text. The full transcript of *College Success: Two Perspectives* conversation is included in your textbook. Watch, listen to and critique the conversation by completing the Conversation Analysis. You can compare your response to the authors by clicking on the Submit button at the end of the form.

Websites of Interest

The following URLs are maintained and updated on the *Everyday Encounters* web site, accessible through http://www.thomsonedu.com. We recommend you begin your web searches at this site to ensure that the links listed below are still active.

Name: Color Affect
Developers: ThinkQuest
Brief Description: Includes information and activities on the effects of color, addressing topics such as how it affects appetite, mood, personality, and the healing process.
URL: http://library.thinkquest.org/TQ0310730

Name: Interpersonal Perception and Communication Lab
Developer: Interpersonal Perception and Communication Laboratory, Harvard University
Brief Description: This web site is a center of research aimed at understanding the ways in which social factors interplay with perception, cognition, and behavior.
URL: http://www.wjh.harvard.edu/~na/

Name: Optics and Visual Perception
Developer: James B. Calvert; University of Denver
Brief Description: Has links to information on optics and visual perception including the senses, nature of illusions, and optical illusions.
URL: http://www.du.edu/~jcalvert/optics/ophom.htm

Name: Risk Perception and Communication

Developer: The Universal Library, Carnegie Mellon University
Brief Description: This site provides papers on risk perception and communication.
URL: http://sds.hss.cmu.edu/risk

Name: Communication, Cognition, and Community
Developer: David C. Smith, University of Washington, published in *Orange*
Brief Description: An article in *Orange: An Online Journal of Technical Communication and Information Design* that links cognitive processes, communication, and human community.
URL: http://tc.eserver.org/orange/2-1/dsmith.htm

Name: Social Cognition Paper Archive and Information Center
Developer: Eliot R. Smith, Purdue University
Brief Description: A searchable archive of papers, abstracts, and presentations on social cognition.
URL: http://www.indiana.edu/~soccog/scarch.htm

Self Test

Multiple Choice

_____ 1. Which of the following is NOT a cognitive schemata used to organize perception?

    A.   prototypes
    B.   personal constructs
    C.   attributions
    D.   stereotypes

_____ 2. Pat says, "I didn't get the job, but it wasn't because I messed up the interview. The interviewer asked really difficult questions and all of my preparation couldn't have prepared me." Pat's explanation for not getting the job illustrates

    A.   a self-fulfilling prophecy
    B.   a self-serving bias
    C.   the influence of social roles
    D.   cultural sense making

_____ 3. "Dr. Tucker is the best professor I've ever had." In this statement, Dr. Tucker is a

    A.   prototype
    B.   stereotype
    C.   personal construct
    D.   script

_____ 4. "In my experience chat rooms are either really interesting or terribly boring." In this statement, which form of schemata is the person is using to organize chat rooms?

A. prototypes
B. personal constructs
C. stereotypes
D. scripts

_____ 5. Which of the following is NOT an influence on perception?

A. inherent meaning
B. culture
C. cognitive ability
D. self

True/False

_____ 6. Perception consists of three continuous, blended processes.

_____ 7. According to constructivism, we organize perceptions by applying schemata.

_____ 8. People who are cognitively complex tend to be less person-centered than people who are less cognitively complex.

_____ 9. The qualities of that which we observe influences the stimuli we select to notice.

_____ 10. A self-serving bias aids in the process of perceiving.

_____ 11. When interpreting that which we perceive, we assign the intrinsic meaning in the phenomena.

Essay

12. Explain the selection part of human perception and, specifically, explain how culture influences what we select to notice. Give an example of how selection influences our communication with others.

13. Using a specific example, explain and illustrate the ladder of abstraction. Your answer should demonstrate clearly how the ladder of abstraction pertains to interpersonal communication.

14. Using a specific example of a time when you misperceived a situation, name and explain how at least three of the guidelines would have helped you perceive the situation more accurately.

15. Differentiate between person-centeredness and empathy by using an example to illustrate the differences.

Personal Reflections

1. Describe the steps in the abstraction process that you followed in a particular instance. Be sure to identify each inferential move and analyze what was eliminated with each step up the ladder of abstraction.

2. Analyze the attributional patterns you use to explain, first, a mean or disappointing behavior by a good friend and, second, by someone whom you do not like. Analyze how differences in your feelings about the two individuals affect your attributional tendencies.

3. Identify a situation where stereotypes (as a schemata used in organizing perceptions) are useful and helpful in a communication situation. Next, identify a situation where that same stereotype becomes unproductive and perhaps damaging.

Chapter 4:   The World of Words

I.   Our language and many of our nonverbal behaviors are symbolic.

    A.   Symbols are <u>arbitrary</u>; there is no natural connection between the symbol and what it represents so at any point in time, the symbol or what it represents could change. An example of a symbol whose meaning has changed over the course of time is _____

        _____

        _____.

    B.   Symbols are <u>ambiguous</u> because we have unique individual experiences; there is a range of meanings on which most members of a culture agree. An example of a time when I interpreted a symbol differently than someone else is _____

        _____

        _____.

    C.   Symbols are not tangible or concrete—the are abstract; we do not touch the symbols we use the same way we may touch the things (e.g., a chair or computer) they represent.

II.   The principles of verbal communication give us an understanding of how symbols work.

    A.   Because language and culture are intricately connected, we learn a set of values, perspectives, and beliefs when we learn to speak or read. Growing up, I learned that _____ indicated we value _____

        _____.

    B.   Because there are no single definitions for symbols, we must interpret them in the context of the present interaction to attach meaning.

C. Communication rules help us develop shared understandings of what is happening in a particular interaction.

 1. Regulative rules help us manage the when, how, where, and with whom we talk about certain things. A regulative rule I usually follow is _____

 _____ .

 2. Constitutive rules define what messages mean, or what communication is expected, in a particular situation. For me, the following behaviors constitute good student:_____

 _____ .

D. Punctuation creates outer limits for what constitutes the beginning and ending of an interpersonal interaction. An example of a time when punctuation differences created a misunderstanding is _____

 _____ .

 1. A common pattern of conflict involving two people punctuating interaction differently is the demand-withdraw cycle.

 2. Punctuation depends on subjective perceptions.

III. The ability to use and understand symbols has an impact on the lives we lead.

A. We use symbols to define experiences, people, relationships, feelings, and thoughts.

 1. The names or labels we attach to people, objects, or events highlight some aspects and de-emphasize others.

2. Our names or labels can highlight just one aspect of a person, object, or event. An example of a time when I used language to <u>totalize</u> someone is

    _____

    _____ .

3. The language we use to define relationships shapes how we view and act in those relationships.

B. Language is value laden and not neutral.

1. The judgments and values that appear in our language choices affect how we view or perceive people, objects, and events. An example of a time when language values affected my perceptions is _____

    _____ .

2. Loaded language strongly affects our perceptions, usually by creating inaccurate negative connotations. An example of <u>loaded language</u> I recently heard is _____

    _____ .

3. Language can degrade others because we are influenced by the names we have for things. An example of degrading language I recently heard is_____

    _____ .

C. Symbols help us organize information and perceptions into categories so that we do not have to remember every aspect of every person, object, and event we encounter.

1. Being able to use language to organize information and perceptions allows for abstract thought.

2. In categorizing information and perceptions, language can stereotype, which distorts thinking. One time that I used language to <u>stereotype</u> is _____

_____.

and my thinking was distorted in this way _____

_____.

D. We can use symbols to label things that have happened in the past, are happening now, and might happen in the future.

E. Symbols allow us to examine our actions so that we can monitor our behavior in a particular situation as well as manage the impression we make on others.

IV. When a group of people share a set of norms about how to talk and the purpose talk serves, they form what is called a speech community.

A. Different speech communities use symbols in different ways.

B. Speech communities are defined by shared ideas of how to communicate, not by geographic locations.

C. Individuals are socialized into gender speech communities at a young age.

V. We can use a set of guidelines for making our verbal communication more effective.

A. Engaging in dual perspective, or walking in the shoes of another person to see the situation as she or he sees it, asks us to create and interpret messages with both our view and the other's view in mind. An example of a time when I should have used <u>dual perspective</u> is _____

_____.

B.   Recognize that starting sentences with "I" instead of "You" leads us to take responsibility for our thoughts and feelings rather than blaming others for them. An example of a time when owning my thoughts and feelings would have been more effective is _____

_____.

C.   Respecting what others say about their thoughts and feelings allows us to be confirming rather than disconfirming them, and helps us engage in dual perspective. An example of a time when I should have used this guideline is _____

_____.

D.   Because symbols are arbitrary, ambiguous, and abstract, we need to find ways to make our communication more accurate and concrete as is necessary for the situation at hand. An example of a time when my communication lacked clarity and/or accuracy is

_____

_____.

1.   Awareness of the levels of abstraction can help make our communication more accurate.

2.   Using qualifying language reminds us of the limitations of a message.

3.   Indexing reminds us that our evaluations should be applied only to a particular time and situation. An example of when I didn't use indexing was _____

_____.

To use indexing, I would have said _____

_____.

Additional Vocabulary

For each of the terms listed below, generate a personal example that illustrates the concept.

Hate speech_____

_____

I-language _____

_____

Static language _____

_____

Key Concepts

abstract
ambiguous
arbitrary
communication rules
constitutive rules
hate speech
I-language
indexing

Linguistic determinism
loaded language
punctuation
regulative rules
speech community
static evaluation
symbols
totalizing
you-language

Activities

Title	Individual	Partner	Group	Ethno.	Internet/InfoTrac
4.1 Breaking the Rules of Gendered Communication	✓				
4.2 The Personal Nature of Meanings	✓			✓	
4.3 Recognizing Ambiguity in Verbal Language	✓				
4.4 Good Enough to Eat			✓		
4.5 Punctuation in Practice	✓				
4.6 Understanding Communication Rules	✓				
4.7 Learning to Use I-Language	✓				
4.8 Reducing the Abstractness of Language	✓				
4.9 Practicing Using Qualified Language	✓				
4.10 Guarding Against Static Language	✓				
4.11 Identifying Sexist and Racist Language	✓				✓
4.12 What is Appropriate Workplace Behavior?	✓				✓

Name _____

Activity 4.1: Breaking the Rules of Gendered Communication

<u>Purposes</u>: To increase your awareness of how gender socialization shapes your verbal communication; To increase your insight into others' perceptions of verbal communication that is and is not appropriate for each sex.

<u>Instructions</u>:

1. Refresh your understanding of gender cultures by reviewing *Gender Speech Communities* in your textbook.

2. Select a social prescription for how your sex is supposed to communicate verbally and deliberately violate that prescription in your interactions with others for one day.

3. Record how others respond to your violation of a gender prescription for verbal behavior.

4. Record how you feel when you violate the prescription and when others respond to your violation.

<u>Example</u>

I chose to break the prescription that women should be empathic by giving only minimal responses and not emotional responses when people talked to me. I kept it up even when my best friend told me about a problem she was having.

Several people asked me if I was sick or angry. When I said I wasn't, they said that I surely was acting cold. My best friend said that I was acting like I didn't care about her.

I felt really weird not responding emotionally to other people. Also, I felt bad when others criticized me, because I felt like I was letting them down by not being my usual empathic self. But when I reflected further, a part of me felt like it isn't fair that women are expected to always be caring, empathic, and all that stuff.

Name _____

Activity 4.2: The Personal Nature of Meanings

Purpose: To provide you with concrete examples of the variations in meanings for words among people.

Instructions:

1.   Select 7 people who are diverse. They should represent a range of ages, sexes, political leanings, races, and so forth.

2.   Ask each person to tell you what each of the 4 terms listed below means to her or him. Record the answers.

3.   With others in your class, discuss the variations in meanings for the "same words."

Feminism	Affirmative Action	Alcoholic	Conflict
Person 1			
Person 2			
Person 3			
Person 4			
Person 5			
Person 6			
Person 7			

Name _____

Activity 4.3: Recognizing Ambiguity in Verbal Language

Purpose: To provide you with concrete examples of ambiguous verbal symbols.

Instructions: For each of the statements below, write 2 distinct ways it might be interpreted.

A.   That is one bad woman.
        Interpretation 1:

        Interpretation 2:

B.   How is your grass?
        Interpretation 1:

        Interpretation 2:

C.   Are you straight?
        Interpretation 1:

        Interpretation 2:

D.   This is very heavy.
     Interpretation 1:

     Interpretation 2:

E.   It's really hot in here.
     Interpretation 1:

     Interpretation 2:

F.   I don't want you to hit on me.
     Interpretation 1:

     Interpretation 2:

Name _____

Activity 4.4: Good Enough to Eat

Purpose: To increase awareness of how language is used to shape perceptions.

Instructions

1. Get together with 5 or 6 other students in your class. Assign each member of your group 3 local restaurants that he or she will study. Make sure that your group includes restaurants of different types (fast food, expensive, etc.).

2. Each member of the group should go the 3 assigned restaurants and ask for a menu. Many restaurants have take-out menus. If a restaurant doesn't have a take out menu, you might ask to borrow a menu to photocopy and then return it.

3. When all members of your group have collected their menus, meet and discuss the language used to describe foods.

As guidelines for your discussion, use the questions that follow.

1. What, if any, language used in describing entrees refers to taste, texture, and other features that contribute to dining pleasure?

2. What, if any, language used in describing entrees emphasizes the health values of the entrees? For example, are entrees described as "low fat," "nutritional," "healthy," "low calorie," and so forth?

3. What, if any, language used in describing entrees emphasizes value? For example, are menu items described as "bargains," "specials," "super buys," and so forth?

4. What differences can you identify in the menu language of expensive restaurants and fast food eateries? Which of the above 3 emphases is most pronounced for different kinds of restaurants?

Name _____

Activity 4.5: Punctuation in Practice

<u>Purpose</u>: To increase your sensitivity to different ways that communication might be punctuated.

<u>Instructions</u>: If you need to refresh your knowledge of punctuation, review *Punctuation Shapes Meaning* in your textbook.

Read the dialogue between Ann and Max that appears below. Then write a description of how Ann seems to punctuate the interaction and a second description of how Max appears to punctuate the interaction.

Max: You seem awfully quiet tonight. Are you okay?

Ann: Hardly (said in a sarcastic voice).

Max: You sound angry.

Ann: Brilliant deduction on your part.

Max: Are you angry with me?

Ann: A second brilliant deduction.

Max: But I just got home--literally just walked in the door. How could I have done anything to make you angry?

Ann: My, you have a short memory.

Max: Cut the sarcasm, will you? My memory is fine. What's the matter with you?

Ann: The "matter with me," as you call it, is our discussion this morning when we were getting ready to go to work.

Max: Yeah. What about it?

Ann: I can't believe you've forgotten how nasty you were. I said I wanted to go back to school next year and you said we couldn't afford it, like that ended the issue.

Max: That's what you're mad about now? We resolved that issue nearly 10 hours ago.

Ann: I didn't. It's not resolved for me.

Ann's punctuation of the interaction:

Max's punctuation of the interaction:

Name _____

Activity 4.6: Understanding Communication Rules

<u>Purpose</u>: To increase your awareness of communication rules.

<u>Instructions</u>: For each of the statements listed below, indicate whether it expresses a constitutive or a regulative communication rule. If you need to refresh your understanding of these two kinds of rules, review *Communication is Rule Guided* in your textbook. In the blanks on the left, place an R if the statement expresses a regulative rule and a C if it expresses a constitutive rule of communication.

_____ 1. Don't talk when you have food in your mouth.

_____ 2. Never engage in conflict in front of others.

_____ 3. True friends listen to what each other says.

_____ 4. It's impolite to interrupt others when they are speaking.

_____ 5. Good buddies don't reveal confidences.

_____ 6. Look at your elders when they speak to you so that you show you respect them.

_____ 7. Children should not speak back to parents.

_____ 8. It's thoughtful to ask others what is going on in their lives.

Answers: Items one, two, four, and seven express regulative rules. Items three, five, six, and eight express constitutive rules.

Name _____

Activity 4.7: Learning to Use I-Language

Purpose: To give you experience in using I-language.

Instructions: If you don't remember what I-language is, review *Own Your Feelings and Thoughts* in your textbook. Read each of the 10 statements below. Each one relies on you-language. Rephrase each statement so that it is expressed using I-language.

Example

Your stubbornness makes me angry.

Rephrasing: I get angry when you are stubborn.

1.   You are so arrogant.

         Rephrasing:

2.   You embarrassed me in front of my friends.

         Rephrasing:

3.   You make me feel guilty.

         Rephrasing:

4.   You get me so upset that I forget things.

         Rephrasing:

5.   You're so inconsiderate of me.
      Rephrasing:

6.   You're very loving.
      Rephrasing:

7.   You're insensitive.
      Rephrasing:

8.   You're so understanding about my situation.
      Rephrasing:

9.   You really are self-centered.
      Rephrasing:

10.   You're very helpful when I talk to you about problems.
      Rephrasing:

Activity 4.8: Reducing the Abstractness of Language

Purposes: To increase your ability to recognize highly abstract language, and to increase your skill in reducing the abstractness of language.

Instructions: If you wish to refresh your understanding of abstraction in language, reread *Strive for Accuracy and Clarity* in your textbook. Each of the statements below is expressed in highly abstract language, which increases the chances of misunderstanding between communicators. Rephrase each statement so that it is less abstract and more clear.

Example

This course is conceptually difficult.

Rephrasing: This course requires students to learn a great many new concepts and to understand how they relate to one another.

1.   Edward always finds something critical to say.

        Rephrasing:

2.   The American concept of freedom is diminishing.

        Rephrasing:

3.   Most people have lost any sense of personal responsibility.

        Rephrasing:

4.   Let's try to keep our trip from getting too expensive.

        Rephrasing:

5.   I wish you would be more responsible.

        Rephrasing:

6.   I'd like for us to be better friends.

        Rephrasing:

7.   Politicians are dishonest.

        Rephrasing:

Name _____

Activity 4.9: Practicing Using Qualified Language

Purpose: To give you experience in using qualified language.

Instructions: If you wish to refresh your understanding of qualified language, review *Strive for Accuracy and Clarity* in your textbook. Below are 10 statements that are unqualified. Each statement is very broad generalization. In the space below each statement, write a rephrased statement that is more qualified.

Example

Politicians are crooks.

Rephrasing: Some politicians sometimes engage in illegal acts.

1.   You never listen to me.
      Rephrasing:

2.   Bureaucrats just follow rules; they never think for themselves.
      Rephrasing:

3.   Republicans don't care about poor people.
      Rephrasing:

4.   Professors expect too much of students.
      Rephrasing:

5.   Men are much more aggressive than women.

Rephrasing:

6.   Required courses are boring.

Rephrasing:

7.   Children shouldn't be allowed to watch commercial television.

Rephrasing:

8.   Women's maternal instincts make them more nurturing than men.

Rephrasing:

9.   Fraternities care more about partying than anything else.

Rephrasing:

10.   You are untrustworthy.

Rephrasing:

Name _____

Activity 4.10: Guarding Against Static Language

Purpose: To give you practice in recognizing and correcting static language.

Instructions: If you don't recall what static language is, review *Strive for Accuracy and Clarity* in your textbook. Listed below are 10 statements that include static language. Rephrase each statement to qualify it in terms of specific times, events, and/or situations.

Example

Marion is irresponsible.

Rephrasing: Marion was irresponsible about returning the sweater he borrowed from me.

1.   Aaron is selfish.
       Rephrasing:

2.   Emily is very supportive.
       Rephrasing:

3.   Dr. Dowler is not interested in talking with students.
       Rephrasing:

4.   Andy cares more about how a woman looks than what kind of personality and values she has.
       Rephrasing:

5. Aimee is immature.
   Rephrasing:

6. Pat can't be relied on to complete assignments.
   Rephrasing:

7. I am stupid.
   Rephrasing:

8. Kim is a real gossip.
   Rephrasing:

9. American cars are poorly made.
   Rephrasing:

10. You are disrespectful of your parents.
    Rephrasing:

Name _____

Activity 4.11: Identifying Sexist and Racist Language
(With InfoTrac-College Edition)

Purpose: To increase awareness of language that may be perceived as sexist or racist by some people.

Instructions:

1.   Read over the 10 sentences below. For each one indicate whether you think it includes language that is sexist or racist by writing an S for sexist or a R for racist in the blank at the left. If you think a sentence is neither sexist nor racist, write nothing in the blank.

2.   For any sentence that you think contains sexist or racist language, write out a revised sentence that avoids sexism and racism.

3.   Compare your answers with those of others in your class.

4.   Search InfoTrac-College Edition for keywords "sexism and language" and "racism and language." Share examples of articles that you find with others in your class.

Example

_____   E.   I now pronounce you man and wife.

Revision: *I now pronounce you husband and wife.*

_____   1.   The waitress took our order.

Revision:

_____   2.   He's the black sheep in the family.

Revision:

_____   3.   Anne is a woman doctor.

Revision:

_____ 4.   It's okay to tell white lies.

Revision:

_____ 5.   Edward babysat his son while his wife was away on business.

Revision:

_____ 6.   Good guys wear white hats.

Revision:

_____ 7.   A lot of Asians are really just like regular people.

Revision:

_____ 8.   She's in a black mood--stay away from her until she gets over it.

Revision:

_____ 9.   The partners in the law firm are Mr. Thompson, Mr. Flagler, Mr. Winstead, and Emily.

Revision:

_____ 10.   Asians are so indirect and deferential.

Revision:

Name _____

Activity 4.12: What is Appropriate Workplace Behavior?
(Using the WWW)

<u>Purpose</u>: To learn about appropriate and inappropriate behaviors in the workplace.

<u>Instructions</u>: Visit the following web site and take the quiz on behaviors that are considered appropriate and inappropriate for the work place:
http://www.workrelationships.com/site/quiz/

After you take the quiz, read the answers to the quiz. Then, make a list of regulative and constitutive rules that guide particular behaviors from the quiz.

Behavior	Regulative Rule	Constitutive Rule
Telling a gender-based joke.	Can be inappropriate in the work place even if it is targeted toward the teller's own gender.	Gender-based jokes can count as hurtful communication.

1.

2.

3.

4.

5.

Using Your *Everyday Encounters* Premium Website

Use your *Everyday Encounters* premium website for quick access to the electronic study resources that accompany this text. The *Everyday Encounters* web site offers an interactive version of many of the activities in this chapter. You can complete these activities online and submit them electronically to your instructor. All of the web links included in this chapter as well as in the accompanying main text chapter are maintained on the web site, accessible through http://www.thomsonedu.com.

Included on the website is access to the Continuing the Conversation video scenario and questions featured in this chapter. Watch, listen to, and analyze the Continuing the Conversation case featuring *Ed Misses the Banquet* included at the end of Chapter 4 in your main text. The full transcript of *Ed Misses the Banquet* conversation is included in your textbook. Watch, listen to and critique the conversation by completing the Conversation Analysis. You can compare your response to the authors by clicking on the Submit button at the end of the form.

Websites of Interest

The following URLs are maintained and updated on the *Everyday Encounters* web site, accessible through http://www.thomsonedu.com. We recommend you begin your web searches at this site to ensure that the links listed below are still active.

Name: Do's and Don'ts of Inclusive Language
Developer: Media Task Force, Honolulu County Committee on the Status of Women Brief Description: This web page discusses the do's and don'ts on using inclusive language.
URL: http://www.hcc.hawaii.edu/intranet/committees/FacDevCom/guidebk/teachtip/inclusiv.htm

Name: Verbal and Nonverbal Exercise
Developer: National Adult Literacy Database
Brief Description: This page provides an exercise to demonstrate the differences between verbal and nonverbal communication in the workplace.
URL: http://www.nald.ca/clr/wkplace/page43.htm

Name: TechDictionary.com
Developer: TechDictionary.com and a lengthy list of international contributors
Brief Description: This website allows you to search by term or keyword; includes chat terms and emoticon meanings.
URL: http://www.techdictionary.com/

Name: Netiquette Guidelines

Developer: Sally Hambridge, Intel Corporation
Brief Description: This web site provides guidelines and rules for use of the internet, or netiquette.
URL: http://www.dtcc.edu/cs/rfc1855.html

Name: Chat Rooms
Developer: FOLDOC -- Free Online Dictionary of Computing
Brief Description: This web site provides explains internet chat and chat rooms.
URL: http://wombat.doc.ic.ac.uk/foldoc/foldoc.cgi?chat

Name: SYMBOLS.com
Developer: HME Media.
Brief Description: SYMBOLS.com is an online encyclopedia of graphic symbols and "contains more than 1,600 articles and 2,500 Western signs in which their histories, uses, and meanings are thoroughly discussed. The signs range from ideograms carved in mammoth teeth by Cro-Magnon men, to hobo signs and subway graffiti."
URL: http://www.symbols.com/

Name: American Sign Language Browser
Developer: Michigan State University Communication Technology Library
Brief Description: This site teaches people how to produce certain signs through the use of Quick Time videos. Sign language constitutes symbolic communication, though not through verbal means.
URL: http://commtechlab.msu.edu/sites/aslweb/browser.htm

Name: EFF "Censorship - `Hate-speech` & Discrimination" Archive
Developer: Electronic Frontier Foundation
Brief Description: A small archive of press releases, articles, papers, as well as related on-site and off-site resources, focusing on hate speech.
URL: http://www.eff.org/Censorship/Hate-speech_discrimination/

Name: Appropriate Workplace Behavior Quiz
Developer: WorkRelationships, Inc.
Brief Description: A 15-item quiz on appropriate and inappropriate workplace behavior. The main website, www.workrelationships.com, also includes articles on workplace behavior.
URL: http://www.workrelationships.com/site/quiz/

Self Test

Multiple Choice

_____ 1. Because symbols are NOT _____, the meanings of words can change over time.

    A.   arbitrary
    B.   ambiguous
    C.   abstract
    D.   absolute

_____ 2. "Do not interrupt when others are speaking." This is an example of a(n) _____ rule.

    A.   constitutive
    B.   regulative
    C.   punctuative
    D.   abstractive

_____ 3. "Paying attention when others speak is a sign of respect," is an example of a(n) _____ rule

    A.   constitutive
    B.   regulative
    C.   punctuative
    D.   abstractive

_____ 4. When we overlook many aspects of a person and define the person only by a single aspect of her or his identity, we are:

    A.   organizing.
    B.   engaging in dual perspective.
    C.   totalizing.
    D.   stereotyping.

_____ 5. The statement, "When I get out of school, I want to go to Nepal," is an example of:

    A.   using symbols to define.
    B.   using symbols to organize.
    C.   engaging in hypothetical thought.
    D.   engaging in punctuation.

_____ 6.   Whorf and Sapir proposed the idea of _____ , which means that language influences the views of a culture, and cultural behaviors and attitudes are reflected in language.

   A.   enculturated symbols
   B.   language as culture
   C.   subjective reflexivity
   D.   linguistic determinism

True/False

_____ 7.   When Maria said, "You make me so mad," she is taking responsibility for her feelings.

_____ 8.   Effective communication respects others for their thoughts and emotions even when they disagree.

_____ 9.   Speech communities are defined by geographical locations.

_____ 10.   Static evaluations focus only on what is negative about a person.

_____ 11.   Language is a value-laden system of symbols.

_____ 12.   The demand-withdraw pattern of punctuation occurs infrequently among couples.

Essay

13.   Explain why symbols allow human beings to live, think, and feel in ways that would not be possible if we were not symbol users.

14.   Explain the importance of owning our own feelings and thoughts. Give an example of how we can accomplish this with the language we use.

15.   Name a speech community based on something other than gender. Compare and contrast the language usage you would expect in its various cultures.

16.   How would you explain to an outsider the communication rules from the speech community in which you grew up?

Personal Reflections

1. Analyze what happened, and how you felt, when you violated the verbal communication rules for your gender.

2. Attend a religious service in a church, synagogue, or temple that is attended primarily by individuals whose race differs from yours. Do not take notes or otherwise appear disrespectful while in the service, but do observe the communication of both leaders and the congregation. Afterward, analyze how communication differs between it and the religious service with which you are most familiar.

3. Describe verbal communication between you and a close friend or romantic partner of the other sex. Analyze the extent to which you and the other person follow patterns typical of women and men in general.

4. Identify at least one regulative and constitutive rule for interacting in face-to-face situations, and one of each type of rule when communicating via e-mail. Reflect on how you learned each of these rules.

Chapter 5:   The World Beyond Words

I.   Nonverbal and verbal communication are both similar to and different from each other.

    A.   Four similarities exist between the two types of communication.

        1.   Nonverbal messages are symbolic, arbitrary, ambiguous, and abstract.

        2.   Different cultures share rules that help us understand what types of nonverbal communication are appropriate as well as what different nonverbal messages mean. For me, touching someone is appropriate when _____

                _____;

                If a stranger touches me, it means_____

                _____

        3.   Nonverbal communication may be intentional or unintentional. An example of a time when I used nonverbal communication intentionally today is _____

                _____

        4.   The culture in which we grew up teaches how, when, and where we use nonverbal codes. An example of a nonverbal code that I used when I was younger and use much less or not at all today is _____

                _____

    B.   Three differences exist between verbal and nonverbal communication.

        1.   Generally, people believe nonverbal communication more than they believe verbal communication, particularly if the two messages contradict each other.

An example of a time when I trusted the nonverbal message more than the verbal message is _____

_____

2.   Nonverbal communication is not limited to a single channel. When I am outside, the nonverbal channel that is most likely to operate is _____

_____

3.   Nonverbal communication does not have distinct starting and ending points.

II.   Four principles guide our understanding of nonverbal communication.

A.   Nonverbal and verbal communication work together by having the nonverbal message repeat, emphasize, complement, contradict, or substitute for the verbal message.

B.   Nonverbal cues also help regulate the flow of interaction between people. An example of a time when I used nonverbal communication to regulate the conversation is _____

_____

C.   Nonverbal messages also tend to emphasize the relational level of meaning in an interaction; these include responsiveness, liking, and power. An example of a nonverbal message that indicates responsiveness for me is _____

_____.

An example of a nonverbal cue that indicates liking for me is _____

_____.

An example of a nonverbal cue that indicates power to me is _____

_____

    D.   Nonverbal communication reflects and expresses culture, which means that we learn nonverbal communication over time.

III.   There are nine basic types of nonverbal communication.

    A.   <u>Kinesics</u> refers to all of our body and facial expressions. My favorite nonverbal kinesic message is _____ and it indicates _____ to those around me.

    B.   <u>Haptics</u> is the technical term we use to refer to our touching behaviors. In   situations, I am most likely to use touch to communicate _____

    C.   <u>Physical appearance</u> messages are frequently the first way we form perceptions of others when we meet them. For me, the most important aspect of physical appearance in a potential romantic partner is _____

    D.   <u>Artifacts</u> are personal objects that we use to indicate to others important information about our self. The most revealing artifact in my life is _____ _____

    E.   <u>Environmental factors</u> are aspects of the communication context which influences how we act and feel. The environmental factors in the classroom we use for this class indicate _____ to me.

    F.   <u>Proxemics</u> is the technical term for space and how we use it. Where I live, I/we use space to indicate _____

G.   How we use and value time is the study of <u>chronemics</u>. For me, being late usually indicates _____ ; I tend to arrive for class _____ minutes early/late (circle one).

H.   Messages that we indicate with our voice, beyond the words we use, are called paralinguistics.

I.   Silence is the final type of nonverbal message. I like to use silence to indicate

_____

IV.   Two guidelines help us use and interpret nonverbal communication more effectively.

A.   We need to use monitoring skills. An example of a time when I should have used monitoring to be more effective was _____

_____

B.   We need to exert caution by enacting personal and contextual qualifications. An example of a time when I should have interpreted nonverbal messages more cautiously is _____

_____

Additional Vocabulary

For the term listed below, generate a personal example that illustrates the concept.

Nonverbal communication _____

_____

Key Concepts

artifacts
chronemics
haptics

kinesics
nonverbal communication
paralanguage
proxemics

Activities

Title	Individual	Partner	Group	Ethno.	Internet/InfoTrac
5.1 Breaking the Rules of Gendered Communication	✓				
5.2 Nonverbal Exclusions	✓			✓	
5.3 Portrait of Myself	✓			✓	✓
5.4 Nonverbal Designs	✓			✓	
5.5 Identifying Nonverbal Cues	✓				
5.6 Monitoring Your Nonverbal Communication	✓				
5.7 Sculpting Personal Image with Nonverbal Communication	✓				
5.8 Feng Shui and Forms of Nonverbal Communication	✓				✓

Name _____

Activity 5.1: Breaking the Rules of Gendered Communication

Purposes: To increase your awareness of how gender socialization shapes your nonverbal communication; To increase your insight into others' perceptions of nonverbal communication that is and is not appropriate for each sex.

Instructions

1. Refresh your understanding of gender cultures by reviewing *Nonverbal Communication Often Establishes Relational-Level Meanings* in your textbook.

2. Select a social prescription for how your sex is supposed to communicate nonverbally and deliberately violate that prescription in your interactions with others for one day.

3. Record how others respond to your violation of a gender prescription for nonverbal behavior.

4. Record how you feel when you violate the prescription and when others respond to your violation.

Example

I broke the gendered rule that men don't smile a lot. All day I smiled whenever I saw people, whether or not I felt happy to see them. I got a lot of odd looks from clerks in stores, but the biggest response was from my girlfriend and my roommates. They kept asking me what I was up to and why I was smiling. I told them I just felt good, but they didn't buy that. They kept saying I was up to something. It felt strange to me to smile all the time. Mainly it felt false because I don't always feel happy or like smiling.

Name _____

Activity 5.2: Nonverbal Exclusions

Purpose: To increase awareness of how environmental settings include and exclude social groups.

Instructions: Choose five places to visit: (1) a business office such as a realty company, (2) an administrator's office on your campus, (3) a commercial building such as a bank, (4) a waiting lounge in a hospital or doctor's office, and (5) a conference room in one of the campus buildings. Visit each of the five locations and record answers to the questions below.

1.   How many pictures or paintings of people of color are present?

Business office

Administrative office

Commercial building

Waiting lounge

Conference room

2.   How accessible is the setting to individuals who have disabilities that restrict their mobility?

Business office

Administrative office

Commercial building

Waiting lounge

Conference room

3.   Are rooms identified with Braille and are reading materials in Braille available?

Business office

Administrative office

Commercial building

Waiting lounge

Conference room

4.   How many photographs or paintings of women are present?

Business office

Administrative office

Commercial building

Waiting lounge

Conference room

Processing

Discuss your observations with other students in your class. Are consistent trends in your observations evident? What can you conclude about nonverbal communication of inclusion and exclusion?

Name _____

Activity 5.3: Portrait of Myself
(Using InfoTrac-College Edition)

Purpose: To increase your awareness of the ways in which you use artifacts to personalize your environment.

Instructions: Go to your dormitory room or your room in your home or apartment. Using the form below, list the personal artifacts that you have put there. Do not list any that you didn't choose. Beside each item that you list, explain its significance to you and what it communicates about your identity.

Artifact	Significance/What it Communicates
Example	
Photo of me in Nepal	This photograph reminds me of a very special trek I made in Nepal. It also communicates to others that I am adventurous.
1.	
2.	
3.	
4.	
5.	

6.

7.

8.

9.

10.

Search *InfoTrac-College Edition* keywords "artifacts" to find articles for the personal and cultural significance of artifacts. Bring ideas from these articles to share with the rest of your class.

Name _____

Activity 5.4: Nonverbal Designs

Purpose: To increase your awareness of the ways in which settings influence interaction.

Instructions

1.   Select three restaurants to visit. One should be a very elegant restaurant; one should be an inexpensive fast-food restaurant; and one should be an ethnic restaurant.

2.   Describe the setting of each restaurant by answering the questions in Part A of the form below.

3.   Describe interaction patterns among diners by answering the questions in Part B of the form below.

PART A: DESCRIPTION OF THE SETTING

1.   What is the average distance between tables or booths?

Elegant restaurant

Fast-food restaurant

Ethnic restaurant

2.   How is the restaurant lit (candles, soft side lighting, overhead bulbs, fluorescent lighting)?

Elegant restaurant

Fast-food restaurant

Ethnic restaurant

3.   What kind of music, if any, is playing in the restaurant? Describe the style and tempo of music.

Elegant restaurant

Fast-food restaurant

Ethnic restaurant

4.   How are members of the staff dressed? Notice the receptionist as well as waitpersons. Are they dressed formally or informally; in uniforms or not?

Elegant restaurant

Fast-food restaurant

Ethnic restaurant

5.   Describe the decor of each restaurant? Identify artwork, if any; quality of carpeting; presence of plants and other items.

Elegant restaurant

Fast-food restaurant

Ethnic restaurant

PART B: DESCRIPTION OF INTERACTION PATTERNS

1.   What is the average time that diners spend in each restaurant?

Elegant restaurant

Fast-food restaurant

Ethnic restaurant

2.   How much do diners, in general, look at one another while eating?

Elegant restaurant

Fast-food restaurant

Ethnic restaurant

3.   How loudly do diners talk?

Elegant restaurant

Fast-food restaurant

Ethnic restaurant

4. What is the average number of people in each party?

Elegant restaurant

Fast-food restaurant

Ethnic restaurant

5. How intimate do diners' conversations appear to be, judging from touching, eye behavior, and other nonverbal cues?

Elegant restaurant

Fast-food restaurant

Ethnic restaurant

Name _____

Activity 5.5: Identifying Nonverbal Cues

Purpose: To make you more aware of nonverbal cues that lead you to particular interpretations of others.

Instructions

1. Using the form below, identify two or more nonverbal behaviors that you associate with the states described on the left.

2. When you have competed the form, consider whether the nonverbal behaviors you listed might have meanings other than those you assign to them.

State	Associated Nonverbal Cues

Example

Happiness   Smiling, laughing

1. Anger

2. Lack of interest

3. Arrogance

4.   Boredom

5.   Romantic interest

6.   Fear

7.   Embarrassment

8.   Type A personality

9.   Nervous

10.   Disapproval

Name _____

Activity 5.6: Monitoring Your Nonverbal Communication

<u>Purposes</u>: To heighten your awareness of nonverbal behaviors that others may misinterpret; To assist you in identifying alternative nonverbal behaviors that are consistent with the messages you intend to send to others.

<u>Instructions</u>

1. On the form below, write six statements about you that others have made but that you do not think are accurate descriptions of you.

2. Identify nonverbal behaviors of yours that others may interpret as the basis of their descriptions of you. You may find it useful to ask others for feedback on your nonverbal communication so that you can understand the cues on which they are relying.

3. Identify alternative nonverbal behaviors you might use to decrease the likelihood that others will misinterpret you.

Description of You	Nonverbal Cues	Alternative Nonverbal Cues
<u>Example</u>		
My spouse says I often seem critical when I am listening to her/him.	I wrinkle my brow a lot when I am concentrating, and I don't smile usually.	I could smile more and use head nods to indicate interest and agreement.

1.

2.

Description of You	Nonverbal Cues	Alternative Nonverbal Cues
Example		
My spouse says I often seem critical when I am listening to her/him.	I wrinkle my brow a lot when I am concentrating, and I don't smile usually.	I could smile more and use head nods to indicate interest and agreement.

3.

4.

5.

Name _____

Activity 5.7: Sculpting Personal Image with Nonverbal Communication

Purpose: To highlight the ways in which you use nonverbal communication to project different images of yourself.

Instructions: Using the form below, describe how you would use nonverbal communication, including artifacts, kinesics, and proxemics to project an identity for yourself that is congruent with the goal and situation that are described.

Desired Image and Situation	Appropriate Nonverbal Communication
Example	
Serious professional in a job interview	Wear a suit and dress shoes; offer a firm handshake; keep good eye contact; avoid funky jewelry.
1. Empathic friend in a discussion about a friend's problem	
2. Irate consumer at the complaint desk in a store	
3. Desirable date at a campus mixer	

4.   Responsible student in a conference with a
       professor after doing poorly on an exam

5.   Responsible, respectable citizen after being
       stopped by a patrol officer for speeding

6.   Angry and disappointed person in conversation
       with a friend who betrayed you.

Name _____

Activity 5.8: Feng Shui and Forms of Nonverbal Communication (Using InfoTrac-College Edition)

Purpose: To learn about intersections between nonverbal communication and the Chinese practice of Feng-Shui.

Instructions: Log on to *InfoTrac-College Edition* and retrieve the following article (to get to this article quickly, do an advanced search by clicking on the "PowerTrac" button, and then find the article by author or title):

> Darling, J. (2003, February 10). Medford, Ore.-Area Businesses Try Feng Shui Design. *Mail Tribune*, pITEM03041010.

Read this article about businesses that utilize feng-shui. In the spaces below, note if and how the nine forms of nonverbal communication are discussed in relation to principles of feng shui. In addition, note any nonverbal responses of those who enter the newly-designed spaces.

Kinesics:

Haptics:

Physical Appearance:

Artifacts:

Environmental Factors:

Proxemics:

Chronemics:

Paralanguage:

Silence:

Using Your *Everyday Encounters* Premium Website

Use your *Everyday Encounters* premium website for quick access to the electronic study resources that accompany this text. The *Everyday Encounters* web site offers an interactive version of many of the activities in this chapter. You can complete these activities online and submit them electronically to your instructor. All of the web links included in this chapter as well as in the accompanying main text chapter are maintained on the web site, accessible through http://www.thomsonedu.com.

Included on the website is access to the Continuing the Conversation video scenario and questions featured in this chapter. Watch, listen to, and analyze the Continuing the Conversation case featuring *Doctor and Patient* included at the end of Chapter 5 in your main text. The full transcript of *Doctor and Patient* conversation is included in your textbook. Watch, listen to and critique the conversation by completing the Conversation Analysis. You can compare your response to the authors by clicking on the Submit button at the end of the form.

Websites of Interest

The following URLs are maintained and updated on the *Everyday Encounters* web site, accessible through http://www.thomsonedu.com. We recommend you begin your web searches at this site to ensure that the links listed below are still active.

Name: Six Ways to Improve Your Nonverbal Communication
Developer: Vicki Ritts & James R. Stein
Brief Description: This web page talks about the importance of improving your nonverbal communication in the classroom.
http://www.hcc.hawaii.edu/intranet/committees/FacDevCom/guidebk/teachtip/commun-1.htm

Name: FAQs About Feng Shui
Developer: The American Feng Shui Institute
Brief Description: This site provides answers to frequently asked questions about the ancient Chinese practice of Feng Shui
URL: http://www.amfengshui.com/faq.htm

Name: Empowerment Enterprises: Excellence in Communication and Image
Developer: Empowerment Enterprises
Brief Description: This site explains the relationship between nonverbal communication and workplace effectiveness.
URL: http://www.casualpower.com/

Name: Maternity Fashions for the Workplace

Developer: Baby Center
Brief Description: This web-based article explains rules of workplace dress for women who are pregnant.
URL: http://www.babycenter.com/refcap/722.html

Name: No Tie Zone
Developer: Unknown
Brief Description: Argues that requiring men to wear ties in the workplace is gender discrimination. Includes a link to a BBC News article about a civil servant who is challenging the tie requirement.
URL: http://www.impactweb.com/tie/

Name: Dress Code Information at Business.com
Developer: Business.com
Brief Description: Links to articles and dress code policies in a wide range of organizations.
URL: http://www.business.com/directory/human_resources/workforce_management/employee_manuals_and_policies/dress_codes/

Name: Nonverbal Communication Research Page
Developer: Marvin Hecht, Ph.D.; University of California-Santa Cruz
Brief Description: Includes lists of nonverbal communication researchers, books, and a few online resources.
URL: http://nonverbal.ucsc.edu/

Self Test

Multiple Choice

_____ 1. The three dimensions of relational-level meanings that may be expressed nonverbally are

    A. power, control, and liking
    B. power, liking, and disliking
    C. power, liking, and responsiveness
    D. liking, responsiveness, and disliking

_____ 2. Kinesics refers to

    A. touching and being touched
    B. movements of the face and body
    C. environmental features that affect interaction
    D. personal space

_____ 3. Nonverbal behavior interacts with verbal communication in all but which of the following ways?

A. contradicting
B. highlighting
C. influencing
D. repeating

_____ 4. Nonverbal and verbal communication are different in that nonverbal communication is

A. single-channeled.
B. not perceived as reliable as verbal communication.
C. always intentional.
D. continuous.

_____ 5. The CEO always keeps others waiting for 10 minutes at meetings. He has the power to be late, whereas others don't and they will wait. This is an example of:

A. chronemics.
B. proxemics.
C. paralanguage.
D. kinesics.

_____ 6. Todd makes it a point to sit as close as possible to individuals with high status. Todd's choice of seating position is an example of:

A. chronemics.
B. proxemics.
C. paralanguage.
D. kinesics.

True/False

_____ 7. Nonverbal communication reflects cultural values.

_____ 8. People with high status are more likely to touch people with less status than vice versa.

_____ 9. Synchronicity between people indicates they are using similar symbols to communicate.

_____ 10. Accents are an example of one form of paralanguage.

_____ 11. The use of silence in communication can be perceived as confirming or disconfirming.

_____ 12. Nonverbal communication is better suited to expressing feelings about relationships rather than verbal communication.

Essay

13.   Design an environment that encourages relaxed, friendly interaction among people. Explain decisions you make about nonverbal features of the environment that you believe will contribute to the relaxed atmosphere.

14.   A friend tells you that she or he just bought a book titled "Read Anyone's Nonverbal Communication with 100% Accuracy" and that she or he intends to break the "hidden code" of communication. Based on your study of nonverbal communication, what advice would you give to your friend?

15.   Discuss the guidelines for improving nonverbal communication and give specific examples of how you might incorporate those guidelines into your everyday communication with others.

Personal Reflections

1.   Violate a nonverbal gender prescription. If you are a woman, you might restrain yourself from smiling for 24 hours, staring challengingly at others when you talk with them, or sitting with your legs and arms spread widely. If you are a man, try smiling continuously—whenever you meet people, when you talk with them, etc. Men may also violate masculine nonverbal prescriptions by giving strong eye contact and abundant head nods and other displays of responsiveness when they converse with others. Analyze how you felt violating the nonverbal prescription for your gender and what responses you got from others.

2.   Analyze the artifacts and environment of your room. What do these nonverbal cues communicate about who you are? How does their presence affect your feelings of comfort, identity, and security? What would be different if all of your personal artifacts disappeared?

3.   Observe people in a public environment, such as a shopping mall or a busy restaurant. Distinguish between two people who are friends and two people who are romantically involved based on their nonverbal communication. What types of nonverbal communication did you use to distinguish the two people?

4.   Consider the clothing you wear in different situations, such as in class, at work, attending a religious or spiritual ceremony, etc. How does this affect the image that you present to others? How does wearing different clothing affect how you feel about yourself? Are there any implicit or explicit rules that regulate what types of clothes you wear?

Chapter 6: Mindful Listening

I. Listening is a process that involves our ears, minds, and hearts; hearing is an activity that involves sound waves stimulating our ear drums.

   A. Being mindful involves paying complete attention to what is happening in an interaction at that moment in time without imposing our own thoughts, feelings, or judgments on others.

   B. Hearing is when we receive the sound waves.

   C. To listen, we also need to select and organize the many stimuli that are part of a conversation.

   D. Once we select, take in, and organize the stimuli, we attach meaning to the messages.

   E. As we engage in communication, we use both verbal and nonverbal means to indicate we are listening.

   F. After a particular interaction has ended, remembering what was exchanged is the last part of the listening process.

II. There are two main categories of obstacles or barriers to effective listening. In addition, at times we do not listen at all.

   A. Obstacles within the situation (external factors) are those situational factors we cannot control.

1. <u>Message overload</u> occurs because we cannot take in all communication with the same level of mindfulness. An example of a time when I experienced message overload recently is _____

_____

2. <u>Message complexity</u> occurs when the messages are too detailed, use technical terms, or contain many difficult connections between the various sentence parts. An example of when I tuned out but should not have because of message complexity is _____

_____

3. <u>Noise</u> is any verbal or nonverbal stimuli in the environment that keeps us from being good listeners. An example of noise that occurred in one of my interactions today is _____

_____

B. The other set of listening barriers is those that we as individuals can control (internal factors).

1. <u>Preoccupation</u> happens when we are so caught up in what is happening with us that we forget to pay careful attention to what is happening in our interaction with others. An example of preoccupation in my life occurred when _____

_____

2. <u>Prejudgment</u> happens when we think we know what others are going to say before they say it, or we tune them out because we believe they have nothing to offer. I engaged in prejudgment when I _____

_____

3. <u>Emotionally loaded language</u> can "push our buttons," either positively or negatively, and we end up tuning out the other person. An example of emotionally loaded language is _____

    _____

4. Because effective listening requires so much energy, there are times when a lack of effort (time or energy) hinders us. An example of a time when I didn't put forth the required listening effort is _____

    _____

5. Sometimes we forget that different types of interactions call for different types of listening; similarly, we sometimes forget that people with different experiences have learned different speaking and listening styles.

C. In addition to barriers to listening, there are times when we engage in nonlistening behaviors.

    1. Pseudolistening is when we pretend that we are paying full attention to a communication interaction. An example of a time when I engaged in pseudolistening is _____

        _____

    2. <u>Monopolizing</u> occurs when we are constantly trying to redirect the communication back to ourselves and our concerns without giving others the opportunity to complete their thoughts. A recent example of monopolizing is

        _____

    3. <u>Selective listening</u> happens when we focus only on certain aspects of a conversation, either those with which we do not agree or those that do not

interest us at the moment. I engaged in selective listening when I _____

_____

4. We engage in <u>defensive listening</u> when we assume a message has negative connotations (relational-level meanings) even though the person did not intend to criticize, attack, or be hostile toward us. An example of defensive listening was when I _____

_____

5. When we <u>ambush</u> another person, we listen only for information that will help us attack the other person and/or that person's ideas. An example of ambushing is when _____

_____

6. <u>Literal listening</u> is ignoring the relational level of meaning. I have seen literal listening in _____ situations.

III. In different situations, we listen to accomplish different communication goals.

A. Sometimes we are interested in the pleasure or enjoyment we receive from listening to a particular type of communication. I like to listen to _____ _____ for pleasure.

B. To gather and evaluate information others provide we need to be mindful, control obstacles, ask questions, and create devices to help us remember and organize information. I listen to _____ _____ to gather and evaluate information.

C.   Listening to support others requires that we are mindful, avoid judgment, understand the other person's perspective on the situation, paraphrase what has been said to check the accuracy of our interpretations, use minimal encouragers, ask questions, and support the person even if we do not support the content or ideas expressed. I listen to support others when I _____

_____

IV.   Three listening guidelines reinforce effective practices.

A.   Being mindful involves listening fully to what is happening. An example of a time when my communication would have been more effective if I had been mindful is _____

_____

B.   Adapting our listening to the situation at hand, our goals, the others' goals, and the individuals involved makes us better able to understand and respond appropriately during and after the interaction. An example of a time when I should have adapted my listening is _____

_____

C.   Putting forth the necessary effort to listen actively focuses our attention on the communication and away from the potential distractions or barriers we often encounter. An example of a time when I should have put forth more effort to listen actively is ____

_____

Additional Vocabulary

For each of the terms listed below, generate a personal example that illustrates the concept.

Hearing _____

_____

Mindfulness _____

_____

Responding _____

_____

Paraphrasing _____

_____

Minimal encouragers _____

_____

Key Concepts

ambushing
defensive listening
hearing
listening
listening for information
listening for pleasure
listening to support others
literal listening
mindfulness

minimal encouragers
monopolizing
paraphrasing
pseudolistening
remembering
responding
selective listening

Activities

Title	Individual	Partner	Group	Ethno.	Internet/InfoTrac
6.1 Rumor Clinic			✓		
6.2 Noticing Forms of Ineffective Listening	✓			✓	
6.3 Learning to Paraphrase	✓			✓	
6.4 Identifying Effective Behaviors for Relational Listening	✓			✓	
6.5 Listening to Support Others	✓				✓
6.6 Listening in the Workplace	✓			✓	✓

Name _____

Activity 6.1: Rumor Clinic

<u>Purpose</u>: To demonstrate the ways in which messages are distorted as they are passed along from person to person.

<u>Instructions</u>

1.   Select six people to join you in this experience. They may be other students in your class or friends and acquaintances of yours.

2.   Read the story below and then close this book. Tell what you remember of the story to person 1 and tell that person to relay the story to person 2 and so forth until the message reaches the 6th person.

3.   Write down the exact words that person 6 uses to tell the story. Compare the account given by person 6 with the original one presented below.

Gene thought a lot about what he wanted to do after college, and he finally decided that he would go to law school in order to become a public defender. Last semester Gene sent in applications to 8 law schools. So far, he has received rejections from 3 of them and acceptances from 2 of them. The other 3 schools haven't contacted him one way or the other. The problem Gene faces now is that both of the schools that have accepted him require his answer (yes or no) by the end of the month. The 3 schools he hasn't heard from are higher on his list of preferred schools than the 2 that have accepted him. He's not sure whether to take one of the sure bets or hold out in the hope that he will be accepted by a better school.

Name _____

Activity 6.2: Noticing Forms of Ineffective Listening

Purpose: To give you experience in recognizing forms of ineffective listening in everyday situations.

Instructions: For the next three days pay particular attention to how others listen. Use the form below to record examples of each of the forms of ineffective listening discussed in your textbook.

Listening Form	Situation	Observed Behaviors
Example		
Selective listening	Ad about the dangers of smoking	Person who smokes started talking during the ad to divert attention

Pseudolistening

Monopolizing

Listening Form	Situation	Observed Behaviors
Example		
Selective listening	Ad about the dangers of smoking	Person who smokes started talking during the ad to divert attention

Selective Listening

Defensive Listening

Literal Listening

Name _____

Activity 6.3: Learning to Paraphrase

Purpose: To give you experience in paraphrasing others' communication.

Instructions: For each of the statements below, write a paraphrase that aims to clarify and check perceptions of what others say. Try to paraphrase in ways that reflect both the thoughts and feelings of the person speaking.

Statement	Paraphrase
Example	
I think we're seeing too much of each other.	So you want us to get together less frequently?
1. I really like communication, but what could I do with a major in this field?	
2. I don't know if Pat and I are getting too serious too fast.	
3. You can borrow my car, if you really need to, but please be careful with it. I can't afford any repairs and if you have an accident, I won't be able to drive to D.C. this weekend.	

Name _____

Activity 6.4: Identifying Effective Behaviors for Relational Listening

<u>Purpose</u>: To increase your awareness of specific verbal and nonverbal behaviors that accompany effective listening.

<u>Instructions</u>: Identify an individual whom you consider to be especially effective when listening to support others. Either think back on past situations in which you have observed that individual interacting or observe the person as she or he listens to friends in the next few days. Based on your recollections and/or observations, answer the questions below.

1. What proxemic behaviors contribute to the impression that this person is listening fully? Describe how she or he uses space.

2. What kinesic behaviors does this person use? Describe his or her body posture, facial expressions, and movements when she or he is listening.

3. Does the person use minimal encouragers? If so, identify several that she or he uses.

4. Does the person paraphrase the communication of people to whom she or he listens?

5. How does the person demonstrate support verbally? Be specific in describing phrases and language.

6.   How does the person demonstrate support using nonverbal communication? Be specific in describing behaviors.

7.   What verbal and/or nonverbal behaviors indicate the person is engaging in dual perspective?

8.   Does the person ask questions of the speaker? If so, identify typical questions.

9.   Does the person make judgmental comments?

10.   Does the person interrupt other than to express minimal encouragers?

Summary: Based on your observations of this individual, write a paragraph that provides a profile of effective relational listening behaviors.

Name _____

Activity 6.5: Listening to Support Others
(Using InfoTrac-College Edition)

<u>Purpose</u>: To provide you with experience in listening to support another person and a relationship with that person.

<u>Instructions</u>: Following each statement in the message below, write a response that shows you are listening to support the speaker. Follow the directions for specific kinds of supportive responses.

Speaker: I'm thinking about studying abroad next year.

Minimal Encourager: _____

_____

Speaker: But I've never lived away from my family, and I wonder if I would be okay on my own.

Paraphrase: _____

_____

Speaker: I'm not sure that I'm mature enough to live on my own for a whole year.

Avoiding judgment: _____

_____

Speaker: I guess what most interests me about the idea is the chance to really experience another culture.

Minimal encourager: _____

_____

Search *InfoTrac-College Edition* keywords "listen and support" to find articles on the various uses of these terms in articles. Bring ideas from these articles to share with the rest of your class.

Name _____

Activity 6.6: Listening in the Workplace
(Using the WWW)

Purpose: To learn about the importance of listening in the workplace.

Instructions: Read the following articles on the importance of listening in a work environment (http://www.cnn.com/2001/CAREER/corporateclass/01/25/listening/ and http://www.cnn.com/2001/CAREER/corporateclass/01/18/grief/index.html). List three to five points about workplace listening made by the author. Then, interview three people who have work experience (other classmates, parents, siblings, alumni, etc.) to find out about their experiences with listening in a work context. To what extent do their experiences mesh with the points made in the articles?

Points about Workplace Listening from Articles

1.

2.

3.

4.

5.

Person #1

Person #2

Person #3

Using Your Everyday Encounters Premium Website

Use your *Everyday Encounters* premium website for quick access to the electronic study resources that accompany this text. The *Everyday Encounters* web site offers an interactive version of many of the activities in this chapter. You can complete these activities online and submit them electronically to your instructor. All of the web links included in this chapter as well as in the accompanying main text chapter are maintained on the web site, accessible through http://www.thomsonedu.com.

Included on the website is access to the Continuing the Conversation video scenario and questions featured in this chapter. Watch, listen to, and analyze the Continuing the Conversation case featuring *Online Dating* included at the end of Chapter 6 in your main text. The full transcript of the *Online Dating* conversation is included in your textbook. Watch, listen to and critique the conversation by completing the Conversation Analysis. You can compare your response to the authors by clicking on the Submit button at the end of the form.

Websites of Interest

The following URLs are maintained and updated on the *Everyday Encounters* web site, accessible through http://www.thomsonedu.com. We recommend you begin your web searches at this site to ensure that the links listed below are still active.

Name: Listening Quotations
Developer: International Listening Association
Brief Description: This site displays hundreds of quotations about listening.
URL: http://www.listen.org/pages/quotes.html

Name: Befrienders International Online
Developer: Befrienders International
Brief Description: This site features a comprehensive list of emotional help lines and also offers e-mail support for people who are currently considering suicide.
URL: http://www.befrienders.org/

Name: Listen To Your Co-Workers Article
Developer: CNN.com
Brief Description: A news article about the importance of listening while in a work environment.
URL: http://www.cnn.com/2001/CAREER/corporateclass/01/25/listening/

Name: When Bad Things Happen to Workers
Developer: CNN.com
Brief Description: This article discusses the importance of giving support, rather than advice, when bad things (e.g., substance abuse, family deaths, etc.) happen to people at work.

URL: http://www.cnn.com/2001/CAREER/corporateclass/01/18/grief/index.html

Name: Listening Test
Developer: Joe Zubrick, University of Maine at Presque Isle
Brief Description: This web site is a listening test.
URL: http://maine.maine.edu/~zubrick/listest.html

Name: Guided Listening Activity
Developer: Management Centre Europe
Brief Description: This address provides a guided exercise and information on active listening.
URL: http://www.mce.be/wbt/feedback/comm.htm

Name: Listen Up! Enhancing Our Listening Skills
Developer: HealthQuest, Warren Shepell Consultants Corp.
Brief Description: Newsletter article that explains why we don't listen, describes types of listeners, and provides very general information in improving listening skills.
URL: http://www.warrenshepell.com/articles/listenup.asp

Name: Listening Skills for Managers
Developer: Management-resources
Brief Description: Stresses the importance of listening for managers. Discusses listening techniques, such as paraphrasing.
URL: http://www.management-resources.org/universal.php?c=12&a=52

Self Test

Multiple Choice

_____ 1. Lyle feels overwhelmed by communication coming from people at a meeting he attends. The project leader is talking about the team's task, members are engaged in side-line conversations, and computer graphics are being presented—all at the same time. Lyle is experiencing:

  A. message complexity.
  B. preoccupation.
  C. message overload.
  D. prejudgment.

_____ 2. Edwina goes to a public presentation by an author whose work she has read and of which she disapproves. Before the author begins speaking, Edwina thinks to herself, "I know what he's going to say and I know he is wrong." Edwina's ability to listen effectively is likely to be hampered by:

A.   message complexity.
B.   preoccupation.
C.   message overload.
D.   prejudgment.

_____ 3. Dan listens carefully to what his father says in order to refute his father's ideas. As soon as his father pauses, Dan jumps in and says, "You said three things that you can't support." Dan seems to be engaging in:

A.   ambushing.
B.   defensive listening.
C.   monopolizing.
D.   pseudolistening.

_____ 4. While in her psychology class, Dianne reads over her notes for an upcoming exam in her economics class. She looks up at the psychology professor often and nods her head to indicate she is attentive. Dianne is engaging in:

A.   ambushing.
B.   defensive listening.
C.   monopolizing.
D.   pseudolistening.

_____ 5. While his friend Kurt is speaking, Pat interjects these comments: "go on," "I'm following you," "what happened next?" These are examples of:

A.   showing dual perspective.
B.   expressing support.
C.   minimal encouragers.
D.   paraphrasings.

_____ 6. In listening for information, we should:

A.   express support.
B.   ask questions.
C.   relax and enjoy what the speaker is saying.
D.   interrupt when the message is not clear.

True/False

_____ 7. Women are more likely to listen to the whole of communication than men.

_____ 8. Selective listening is not influenced by culture.

_____ 9. Prejudging others is both limiting and disconfirming.

_____ 10. Engaging in dual perspective requires a person to agree with the other person's perspective.

_____ 11. Mindfulness is the foundation of listening for pleasure, for information, and to support others.

_____ 12. Conversational "rerouting" is steering the conversation away from a touchy subject.

Essay

13. Describe the attitudes and skills that are particularly useful when the goal of listening is to support others.

14. Choose three forms of nonlistening, define each one, and give an example of when you engaged in each form of nonlistening. For each example, discuss the consequences of nonlistening.

Personal Reflections

1. Go to a place on campus where students gather and talk. Find a spot where you can unobtrusively observe and hear conversations between other students. Using the information in Chapter 6 of the textbook, record ineffective listening behaviors that you notice. Record effective listening behaviors that you notice. Analyze how the conversations you overheard were supported or impeded by listening styles and behaviors.

summarize what your interviewee said and relate her or his observations to principles discussed in the textbook.

3. Analyze your own listening effectiveness. Using the textbook to guide you, analyze your strengths and weaknesses in terms of the text's guidelines for effective informational listening and effective relational listening. Identify two listening skills you would like to improve and describe how you plan to develop greater competence in each.

4. Make a list of phrases or quotations to which you are exposed that involve listening (visit http://www.listen.org/pages/quotes.html for ideas). Analyze the cultural values and assumptions implicit in each phrase.

Chapter 7:   Emotions and Communication

I.   How well we communicate emotions influences the depth and quality of our interpersonal relationships.

    A.   Emotional intelligence is being able to recognize and communicate the feelings appropriate and necessary for a given situation or context. A person I know who has a high emotional intelligence is _____;
recently this person exhibited emotional intelligence when he/she _____

_____

    B.   Emotions occur over time because physiology, perceptions, and social experiences influence them.

        1.   A physiological approach to emotion, also known as the organismic view of emotions, suggests that we experience a stimulus that creates a physiological reaction so that we can then experience an emotion. Currently, this view is not widely accepted.

        2.   A perceptual view of emotions suggests that we experience a stimulus that creates our perception of the event and interpretation of the emotion so that we can have a physiological response.

        3.   A cognitive labeling view of emotions suggests that we experience a stimulus that creates a physiological response to which we attach a label so that we can experience an emotion.

        4.   An interactive view of emotions suggests that what we feel and how we express those feelings is intricately tied to our social situation.

a.   <u>Framing rules</u> are guidelines for defining the emotional meaning of situations. For me, the framing rules associated with high school graduation are _____

_____

b.   <u>Feeling rules</u> tell us what we should feel or expect to feel in particular situations based upon our society's values. For me, the feeling rules associated with high school graduation are _____

_____

C.   Emotion work is the time and energy we need to put forth to generate what we believe is a desired outcome in a particular situation. A recent time I engaged in <u>emotion work</u> is

_____

D.   The approach towards emotions we adopt affects our belief that we can (or can't) control our emotions and the feelings we can experience and express in our everyday lives.

II.   There are two related sets of obstacles to effective emotional communication.

A.   Just because we feel an emotion does not mean we express it to others.

1.   Social expectations for Westerners indicate that it is more acceptable for women to express emotions and for men to refrain from expressing most emotions. An example of when I based my choice to express or not express emotions on social expectations is _____

_____

2.   Exposing our emotions to others makes us vulnerable because we do not necessarily know how our disclosures may be used in future interactions. An

example of a time when I based my choice to express or not express emotions on vulnerability is _____

_____

3.   In an effort to protect those about whom we care, we sometimes choose not to express our emotions. An example of a time when I based my choice to express or not express emotions on protecting others is _____

_____

4.   Certain social and professional roles dictate that we not express certain types of emotions.

B.   Just because we express an emotion does not mean that we communicate it effectively.

1.   Abstract statements of feelings do not indicate how we truly feel in a given situation. An example of a time when I expressed my feelings by speaking in generalities is _____

_____

2.   Sometimes we express emotions by indicating that something or someone other than ourselves caused us to feel this way. An example of a time when I expressed my feeling by not owning feelings is_____

_____

3.   Counterfeit emotional language happens when we think we are expressing an emotion and the language we choose does not actually describe what we are feeling. An example of a time when I used counterfeit emotional language is

_____

_____

III.   There are six general guidelines for expressing our emotions more effectively.

A.   We need to identify what we feel before we try to express it to others. An example of a time when I should have identified my feelings first is _____

_____

B.   Choosing how to communicate our emotions involves assessing our current state as well as selecting an appropriate time and place to discuss our emotions. An example of a time when I should have chosen how to express emotions more carefully is _____

_____

C.   Use I-language to express feelings. This reminds us that we own our own emotions and it avoids making others feel defensive. An example of a time when I should have used I-language is _____

_____

D.   Monitoring how we talk to ourselves about our emotions allows us to gain a better understanding of what we are feeling and whether we want to express it to others. An example of a time when I should have monitored my self-talk is

_____

E.   Adopting a rational-emotive approach to feelings focuses attention on destructive thoughts about emotions that harm the self and relationships with others.

F.   We need to respond sensitively to others when they express their feelings, just as we would like them to respond sensitively to us when we express our emotions. An example of a time when I should have responded more sensitively to someone else's expression of emotion is _____

_____

Additional Vocabulary

For each of the terms listed below, generate a personal example that illustrates the concept.

Deep acting _____

_____

Surface acting _____

_____

"The pinch" _____

_____

Feeling Rules _____

_____

Rational-emotive approach to feelings _____

_____

Key Concepts

cognitive labeling view of emotions
counterfeit emotional language
deep acting
emotional intelligence
emotions
emotion work
feeling rules

framing rules
interactive view of emotions
organismic view of emotions
perceptual view of emotions
rational-emotive approach to feelings
surface acting

Activities

Title	Individual	Partner	Group	Ethno.	Internet/InfoTrac
7.1 Identifying Your Emotions and Situations	✓				
7.2 Emotional Intelligence	✓				✓
7.3 Feeling and Framing Rules	✓		✓		
7.4 Expressing Emotions Effectively	✓				
7.5 Naming and Enacting Emotions	✓			✓	
7.6 Emotions Meet Icons	✓			✓	✓
7.7 I/ME Dialogues and Emotions	✓				

Name _____

Activity 7.1: Identifying Your Emotions and Situations

Purpose: To identify your emotions and which situations are appropriate for expressing those emotions.

Instructions

1.   Below is a list of emotions some people experience. On the left of each emotions is a line. If you experience this emotion, place an "X" on the line.

2.   For those emotions you experience, list a situation appropriate for expressing the emotion on the line to the right of the emotion.

Experience Emotion	Emotion	Situation
_____	Anger	_____
_____	Anxiety	_____
_____	Apathy	_____
_____	Depression	_____
_____	Disappointment	_____
_____	Embarrassment	_____
_____	Envy	_____
_____	Gratitude	_____
_____	Guilt	_____
_____	Happiness	_____
_____	Hope	_____
_____	Hopelessness	_____
_____	Insecurity	_____
_____	Jealousy	_____

Experience Emotion	Emotion	Situation
_____	Joy	_____
_____	Loneliness	_____
_____	Passion	_____
_____	Peace	_____
_____	Pressure	_____
_____	Sadness	_____
_____	Security	_____
_____	Shame	_____
_____	Surprise	_____
_____	Suspicion	_____
_____	Sympathy	_____
_____	Tenderness	_____
_____	Uncertainty	_____
_____	Vindictiveness	_____
_____	Weariness	_____
_____	Yearning	_____

What do the emotions you checked and situations you generated say about who you are?

What do the emotions you did not check say about who you are?

For what kinds of situations would expect the remaining emotions to be appropriate?

Name _____

Activity 7.2:Emotional Intelligence (Using InfoTrac-College Edition)

Purpose: To examine your emotional intelligence and how socialization affects it.

Instructions:

1.   Generate a list of emotions you have felt or expect to feel in each of the following situations.

2.   Explain why you think they would be an appropriate emotions for the situation.

3.   What from your personal experiences (interactions with others, interaction with the media–books, television, movies) led you to conclude these emotions were appropriate?

Example Situation	Emotions	Socialization
Birth of a Child	Ecstasy, Joy, Respect, Love, Fear	My religious and educational background taught me about the miracle of life and my parents taught me to be weary of and excited about new situations.

	Situation	Emotions	Socialization
1.	First day of school		
2.	Family vacations/trips		
3.	First day of college		
4.	College social		

	Situation	Emotions	Socialization
5.	Failing a course		
6.	Finding out a close friend is dating the person you desire		
7.	Commitment ceremony/wedding		
8.	Divorce		
9.	Family reunion		
10.	High school reunion		
11.	Break up of a committed romantic relationship		
12.	Death/funeral		

Search *InfoTrac-College Edition* keywords "emotional intelligence" to find the most recent articles on how emotional intelligence is being applied to workplace contexts. Bring ideas from these articles to share with the rest of your class.

Name _____

Activity 7.3: Feeling and Framing Rules

Purpose: To define the impetus for personal feeling and framing rules.

Instructions: List all of the feeling and framing rules you can think of that are proposed by or prescribed for you sex.

Feeling Rules   Framing Rules

1.

2.

3.

4.

5.

6.

7.

8.

9.

10.

Activity 7.4: Expressing Emotions Effectively

<u>Purposes</u>: To practice expressing emotions effectively. To identify ineffective expressions of emotion.

<u>Instructions</u> For each of the statements below, identify why it is an ineffective strategy for expressing emotions and rewrite the statement to be a more effective expression of emotion.

<u>Example</u>

Expression	Form of Ineffective Expression	More Effective Expression
"I'm angry"	Speaking in Generalities	"I'm frustrated with myself because I knew the answer to that question and could not recall it during the exam."

Expression	Form of Ineffective Expression	More Effective Expression
"The instructor made me mad."		

"You're a great person."

"I'm sad."

Example		
Expression	Form of Ineffective Expression	More Effective Expression
"I'm angry"	Speaking in Generalities	"I'm frustrated with myself because I knew the answer to that question and could not recall it during the exam."

"I feel good."

"I think we should go to the movies."

"I think we're missing the point."

"I could kill Abhik."

"I've felt better."

Name _____

Activity 7.5: Naming and Enacting Emotions

Purpose: To expand your emotional repertoire, both verbal and nonverbal.

Instructions

1.   Go out and observe approximately 15 to 45 minutes worth of interaction. If you cannot find a suitable place to observe or feel uncomfortable observing people without their knowledge, use a television show or movie for your analysis.

2.   Make a list of the emotions that each person in the interaction expresses.

3.   Generate a list of two alternative verbal ways this emotion could have been expressed and two alternative nonverbal ways this emotion could have been expressed.

Emotion	Verbal Alternatives	Nonverbal Alternatives
1.		
2.		
3.		
4.		
5.		
6.		
7.		
8.		

Name _____

Activity 7.6: Emotions Meet Icons
(Using the WWW)

Purpose: To learn about how emoticons are used.

Instructions: Visit the web site http://www.netlingo.com/smiley.cfm (and related links on this web site) to read about emoticons, or how emotions are expressed graphically in online communication and text messaging. Make a list of the emoticons that you can commonly use, if any, and their meanings in your own email and text messaging communication. Then, survey five people (other students, family, friends, etc.) about what emoticons they most commonly use, if any, when they send email and text messages, and their reasons for doing so. Do you use the same emoticons as others? If not, why not? Considering there are so many possible emoticons to use, consider reasons why people may not use all those available.

Emoticons I Use and Their Meanings

Emoticons Others Use

Person #1

Person #2

Person #3

Person #4

Person #5

Reasons Why People May Not Use A Variety of Emoticons

1.

2.

3.

Name _____

Activity 7.7: I/ME Dialogues and Emotions

Purpose: To consider the connections between I/Me dialogues and emotions.

Instructions: Recall the discussions in Chapter 4 on Mead's I/Me dialogues and 7 on self-talk. We learned that we may not always express emotions (the ME part of the self) we experience (the I part of the self). Below, describe three situations where you did not express an emotion you were experiencing and then list your reasons for not doing so.

Situation Where Emotion Was Experienced, But Not Expressed	Reason(s) For Not Expressing Emotion
1.	
2.	
3.	

Using Your Everyday Encounters Premium Website

Use your *Everyday Encounters* premium website for quick access to the electronic study resources that accompany this text. The *Everyday Encounters* web site offers an interactive version of many of the activities in this chapter. You can complete these activities online and submit them electronically to your instructor. All of the web links included in this chapter as well as in the accompanying main text chapter are maintained on the web site, accessible through http://www.thomsonedu.com.

Included on the website is access to the Continuing the Conversation video scenario and questions featured in this chapter. Watch, listen to, and analyze the Continuing the Conversation case featuring *Damien and Chris* included at the end of Chapter 7 in your main text. The full transcript of Damien and Chris's conversation is included in your textbook. Watch, listen to and critique the conversation by completing the Conversation Analysis. You can compare your response to the authors by clicking on the Submit button at the end of the form.

Websites of Interest

The following URLs are maintained and updated on the *Everyday Encounters* web site, accessible through http://www.thomsonedu.com. We recommend you begin your web searches at this site to ensure that the links listed below are still active.

Name: A-Z Lyrics Universe
Developer: AZLyrics.com
Brief Description: Browse by artist, or search using artist's name, album title, or song title.
URL: http://www.azlyrics.com/

Name: Lyrics.com
Developer: Lyrics.com
Brief Description: This web site contains lyrics to popular songs organized by artist.
URL: http://www.lyrics.com

Name: Smileys and Emoticons
Developer: NetLingo
Brief Description: Smileys and emoticons displayed and defined from A Rose to Yuppie.
URL: http://www.netlingo.com/smiley.cfm

Name: Internet Acronyms Dictionary
Developer: gaarde.org
Brief Description: Acronyms defined from A to Z.
URL: http://www.gaarde.org/acronyms/
Name: Emotion and Nonverbal Communication

Developer: Interpersonal Perception and Communication Laboratory, Harvard University
Brief Description: This site discusses current research projects on emotion and nonverbal communication.
URL: http://www.wjh.harvard.edu/~na/emotion.html

Self Test

_____ 1.   The _____ view of emotions is also called appraisal theory.

      A.   cognitive labeling
      B.   organismic
      C.   interactive
      D.   perceptual

_____ 2.   Management of what we feel inside ourselves is called

      A.   surface acting
      B.   emotional intelligence
      C.   cognitive shaping
      D.   deep acting

_____ 3.   We are most likely to engage in emotion work when we

      A.   think what we are feeling is inappropriate
      B.   want to feel more deeply than we do
      C.   don't feel anything
      D.   have strong emotional reactions to events

_____ 4.   The _____ view of emotions claims that what we feel is shaped by how we label our physiological responses.

      A.   cognitive labeling
      B.   organismic
      C.   interactive
      D.   perceptual

_____ 5.   Which of the following does NOT belong as a process which shapes our emotions?

      A.   perceptions
      B.   cognitive complexity
      C.   language
      D.   physiology

True/False

_____ 6.   We can control how we express feelings.

_____ 7. We tend to experience emotions holistically rather than individually.

_____ 8. Gender socialization does not affect the way we express emotions.

_____ 9. Expressing feelings is always advisable.

_____ 10. Speaking in generalities is an ineffective way to express emotions.

_____ 11. The two processes of what we feel and how we express it are intertwined.

_____ 12. Emotions cannot be expressed nonverbally.

Essay

12. Describe three of the six guidelines for communicating emotions effectively. Give examples of when you applied each of the three guidelines, or explain how each guideline would have helped you communicate your emotions in a particular situation.

13. The textbook talks about four approaches to emotion. Choose one of the approaches and defend why you believe it is the best way of viewing emotions. Provide personal examples to support your choice.

14. Using what you know about the creation of self through communication, describe what you believe are the three most important influences on how you express or do not express emotions. Provide specific examples for each of the influences.

15. Name three emotions you tend to express around your friends. Provide one verbal example and one nonverbal example of how you express these emotions. What influences have taught you to express these emotions in this way?

16. Describe a situation where choosing to express or not express an emotion was made based on ethical decisions.

Personal Reflections

1. Describe one situation in which you did not express your emotions due to concerns for vulnerability or for the need to protect others.

2. Describe the framing and feeling rules that operated in your family. Explain when you were allowed to feel certain emotions and which emotions were expected in specific situations.

3. Emoticons are graphical ways of representing emotions and other nonverbal features in computer mediated communication (CMC). Identify the emoticons you commonly use in your CMC. Reflect on why you limit your use of emoticons to those you identify.

Chapter 8: Communication Climate: The Foundation of Personal Relationships

I.   Four elements contribute to satisfying personal relationships.

      A.   <u>Investments</u> are the contributions (e.g., time, energy, emotions) that we make to relationships without expecting to get them back if the relationship ends; in the most satisfying relationships, everyone feels like the investments made by all involved are roughly equal. My relationship with _____

              _____

              is an example of equal investment.

      B.   <u>Commitment</u> is the personal choice we make to keep a personal relationship alive in the future. An example of how I show commitment in a personal relationship is by _____

              _____

      C.   <u>Trust</u> develops in a relationship as the people involved do what they say they will do and support each other. An example of a relationship in which I did not trust the other person is _____

              _____

      D.   Comfort with <u>relational dialectics</u> which are the opposing forces or tensions that crop up in everyday relational functioning.

            1.   We need to address our desire for independence (autonomy) and interdependence (connection).

2. We need to address our desire for what is familiar or habitual (predictability) and what is new or different (novelty).

3. We need to address our desire for open communication (openness) and privacy (closedness).

4. We can manage these tensions through neutralizing them, selecting one over another, separate one from another into different aspects of our lives, and reframing the tensions by redefining what the tensions mean to us.

II. Different types of communication create supportive and defensive climates in personal relationships.

A. Interpersonal climates occur on a continuum from confirming to disconfirming.

B. Confirming messages recognize that another person exists, acknowledge that another matters to us, and endorse what we believe is true. An example of a confirming message I recently experienced is _____

_____

C. Disconfirming messages deny the person's existence, indicate the other person does not matter to us, and reject another person's feelings or thoughts. An example of a disconfirming message I recently experienced is _____

_____

D. There are six types of communication that create supportive and defensive relational climates.

1. We create supportive climates when we describe behaviors and others; we create defensive climates when we judge or evaluate others.

2. We create supportive climates when we communicate openness to a variety of points of view; we create defensive climates when we use language that indicates there is only one way to view a situation (e.g., it's my way or the highway).

3. We create supportive climates when our communication feels open, honest, and spontaneous; we create defensive climates when our communication feels manipulative, premeditated, and strategic.

4. We create supportive climates when we use communication to find ways of satisfying everyone involved in the interaction; we create defensive climates when we try to control, triumph over, or manipulate others, what they think, and what they do.

5. We create supportive climates when we demonstrate empathy or care about the other person; we create defensive climates when we act in a neutral, detached, or indifferent way.

6. We create supportive climates when we use communication to indicate that all parties are equal; we create defensive climates when we use communication to indicate that one person is superior to another.

III. There are at least six guidelines for building and sustaining healthy relational and communication climates.

A. Monitor our communication so that we use it to create supportive rather than defensive climates. An example of a time when I could have used the information I know now to build or sustain a relationship is _____

_____

B. We need to accept and confirm others while still being honest. An example of a time when I should have been more accepting or more honest is _____

_____

C. We need to make sure we confirm and assert (state what we need, feel, or want without putting ourselves above or below others) ourselves in a relationship. An example of a time when I should have asserted myself in a relationship is

_____

D. We need to self disclose when it is appropriate; use caution when choosing how much, when, and to whom to disclose. An example of a time when I should have disclosed more/less (circle one) is _____

_____

E. Understand that there is not a single mold into which all relationships fit. An example of a time when I should have recognized and respected the diversity in relationships is ___

_____

F. Find ways to respond effectively to criticism. An example of a time when I could have responded more constructively to criticism is _____

_____

Additional Vocabulary

For each of the terms listed below, generate a personal example that illustrates the concept.

Interpersonal climate _____

_____

Self disclosure _____

_____

Autonomy/Connection _____

_____

Predictability/Novelty _____

_____

Openness/Privacy _____

_____

Ethnocentrism _____

_____

Key Concepts

assertion	investment
commitment	relational dialectics
ethnocentrism	self-disclosure
interpersonal climate	trust

Activities

Title	Individual	Partner	Group	Ethno.	Internet/InfoTrac
8.1 Features of Relationships	✓				
8.2 Increasing Your Awareness of Self-Disclosure Risk Levels	✓		✓		
8.3 Changing Windows of Yourself	✓			✓	
8.4 Using Supportive Communication	✓				
8.5 Transforming Defensive Communication into Supportive Communication	✓				
8.6 Distinguishing Aggressive, Assertive, and Deferential Forms of Communication	✓				
8.7 Distinguishing Between Love and Commitment	✓				✓
8.8 Rating the Supportiveness of Communication Climates	✓			✓	
8.9 Recognizing Relational Dialectics	✓				
8.10 Communicating Levels of Confirmation	✓				
8.11 Assertiveness Inventory	✓				✓

Name _____

Activity 8.1: Features of Relationships

Purposes: To allow you to apply research on close relationships to two important relationships in your life; To help you understand the bases of satisfaction in two important relationships in your life.

Instructions

1. To refresh your knowledge of the four features that research indicates characterize satisfying close relationships, read *Elements of Satisfying Personal Relationships* in the textbook.

2. Identify a close friend and a current or past romantic partner. Each person should be one with whom you did or do have a satisfying close relationship.

3. Use forms A and B on the following pages to describe central features of satisfying relationships as they operate in your personal relationships.

FORM A: FEATURES IN FRIENDSHIP

Feature	Presence in Your Relationship

1. Investments
   * What have you invested?

   * What has your friend invested?

2. Commitment
   * How certain are you that the two of you will remain close friends?

   * To what extent do the two of you talk about a shared future or future plans?

3. Trust
   * How much do you feel you can rely on your friend to do what she/he says she/he will do?

   * How much do you count on your friend to look out for you and your welfare?

4. Relational Dialectics

   * How do you manage needs for autonomy and connection?

   * How do you manage needs for novelty and predictability?

   * How do you manage needs for openness and privacy?

FORM B: FEATURES IN ROMANTIC RELATIONSHIP

Feature	Presence in Your Relationship

1. Investments

    * What have you invested?

    * What has your partner invested?

2. Commitment

    *   How certain are you that the two of
          you will together in a romantic relationship?

    *   To what extent do the two of you talk
          about a shared future or future plans?

3. Trust

    *   How much do you feel you can rely on your
          partner to do what she/he says she/he will do?

    *   How much do you count on your partner to look
          out for you and your welfare?

4. Relational Dialectics

    *   How do you manage needs for autonomy
          and connection?

    *   How do you manage needs for novelty and
          predictability?

    *   How do you manage needs for openness
          and privacy?

Name _____

Activity 8.2: Increasing Your Awareness of Self-Disclosure Risk Levels

Purposes: To provide you with an opportunity to compare your perception of the risk level involved with different types of self-disclosure and to compare that with the perceptions of others in your class. Knowing how others feel about the appropriateness of disclosing certain types of information will help you in making appropriate choices when self-disclosing or receiving disclosures from others.

Instructions

Complete the following list of statements according to how you perceive its risk (L=Low risk; M=Moderate risk; H=High risk)

_____ 1.   Your parents' marital status.

_____ 2.   Your academic major

_____ 3.   Your grades

_____ 4.   Your religious affiliation and beliefs

_____ 5.   Your marital or dating status

_____ 6.   Your political affiliation and views

_____ 7.   The details of your sex life

_____ 8.   Your weakness that you most detest

_____ 9.   Your strength that you like most

_____ 10.   Your hopes and dreams for the future

_____ 11.   Your biggest disappointments in the past

_____ 12.   Your own dependencies or vices

_____ 13.   Your biggest accomplishment

_____ 14.   Your biggest failure

Compare your responses with that of your classmates. Listen for the disparity between perceptions of appropriateness of certain topics.

Name _____

Activity 8.3: Changing Windows of Yourself

Purpose: To increase your awareness of how knowledge about yourself that others have changes over the course of a relationship. If you do not recall the textbook's discussion of the Johari Window, review *Self-Disclose When Appropriate* in Chapter 2 before proceeding with this activity.

Instructions

1. Identify a friend or romantic partner with whom you have had a long relationship. For this activity, it's important that you think about a relationship that has endured for quite a while.

2. Recall the early stages of this relationship. You might think about the first 2 or 3 dates with a romantic partner or the first long talks with someone who became a close friend. Fill in Johari Window #1 with content for each pane at the early stage of your relationship.

3. Think back to a mid-point in the relationship's development. It might be when you and a romantic partner first expressed love for each other or when you and a friend took a vacation together. Fill in Johari Window #2 with content for each pane at the mid-point in the relationship.

4. Think about the relationship as it is today. Fill in Johari Window #3 with content for each pane at the current stage in the relationship.

Johari Window #1

Time 1: Early Stage of Relationship

	Known to Self	Unknown to Self
k n o w n t o o t h e r s	Open Area	Blind Area
u n k n o w n t o o t h e r s	Hidden Area	Unknown Area

Johari Window #2

Time 2: Mid-point in the Relationship

	Known to Self	Unknown to Self
k n o w n t o o t h e r s	Open Area	Blind Area
u n k n o w n t o o t h e r s	Hidden Area	Unknown Area

Johari Window #3

Time 3: Current Stage of the Relationship

	Known to Self	Unknown to Self
k n o w n t o o t h e r s	Open Area	Blind Area
u n k n o w n t o o t h e r s	Hidden Area	Unknown Area

Name _____

Activity 8.4: Using Supportive Communication

Purpose: To provide you with concrete experience in creating supportive communication.

Instructions: Following each statement below, write out responses that foster a supportive interpersonal climate. Your responses should follow the directions given below.

Example

Statement: I should have studied harder for the test.

Response: (descriptive)   You don't think you studied enough.

    (empathic)   I know how you feel.

Statement 1: I think Pat is cheating on me.

Response: (provisionalism) _____

_____

    (problem-orientation) _____

_____

Statement 2: I think I need to go on a diet.

Response: (empathy) _____

_____

    (provisionalism) _____

_____

    (equality) _____

_____

_____

<u>Example</u>

Statement: I should have studied harder for the test.

Response: (descriptive)   You don't think you studied enough.

                    (empathic)   I know how you feel.

Statement 3: Do you think it's ever right to tell a lie?

Response: (spontaneity) _____

_____

                  (provisionalism) _____

_____

Statement 4: My counselor suggested that I go on medication to control my depression.

Response: (problem-orientation) _____

_____

                  (description) _____

_____

                  (equality) _____

_____

Name _____

Activity 8.5: Transforming Defensive Communication into Supportive Communication

Purposes: To provide you with concrete examples of communication that cultivates defensiveness; To give you experience in transforming communication that fosters defensive climates into communication that fosters supportive climates.

Instructions: Listed below are 10 statements using language that cultivates defensive communication climates. Following each statement listed below, write out an alternative statement that is more likely to build a supportive communication climate. Follow directions for the type of supportive language to use.

Defensive-producing Language	Supportive Language
Example	
Change evaluation to description	
You are such a whiner.	You seem to be making a lot of complaints lately.

---

1. Change certainty to provisionalism

The right thing to do is crystal clear.

2. Change strategy to spontaneity

Don't you owe me a favor from when I typed that paper for you last term?

Defensive-producing Language	Supportive Language

192

<u>Example</u>

Change evaluation to description

| You are such a whiner. | You seem to be making a lot of complaints lately. |

---

3. Change evaluation to description

You're acting very immaturely.

4. Change control orientation to problem orientation

I think we should move where I have the good job
offer since I'll make a bigger salary than you anyway.

5. Change superiority to equality

I can't believe you got yourself into such a
dumb predicament.

6. Change neutrality to empathy

I don't want to get involved in your disagreement
with your parents.

Name _____

Activity 8.6: Distinguishing Aggressive, Assertive, and Deferential Forms of Communication

Purpose: To increase your awareness of distinctions among aggressive, assertive, and deferential styles of communicating.

Instructions: Listed below are five scenarios that describe a situation and your goal in the situation. For each scenario, write an aggressive, assertive, and deferential statement expressing your goal.

Example

Scenario: You need to study for an examination, but your boyfriend/girlfriend really wants to go out for dinner and a movie.

Aggressive
response: I don't care about your preferences. I'm not going out tonight.

Assertive
response: I'd like to go out tomorrow or this weekend, but I have to study tonight.

Deferential
response: I guess studying isn't really that important. We can go out if you want to.

Scenario 1:   You think your roommate is angry with you, but you have no idea why and she/he denied being angry when you stated your perception. But she/he is acting very distant and unfriendly.

   Aggressive response:

   Assertive response:

   Deferential response

Scenario 2:   One of your close friends asks to borrow your car. Normally, you wouldn't mind lending your car to a friend, but this person has a record of speeding and being careless behind the wheel. You can't afford to have your car wrecked.

    Aggressive response:

    Assertive response:

    Deferential response

Scenario 3:   A close friend asks you about something very personal. You want to show that you trust the friend, but you don't want to discuss this topic--even with a close friend.

    Aggressive response:

    Assertive response:

    Deferential response

Scenario 4:   Ten days ago you lent $20 to one of your co-workers with the understanding that the loan would be repaid within a week. The co-worker has not repaid the money, nor offered any explanation. You need the loan repaid.

Aggressive response:

Assertive response:

Deferential response

Scenario 5:   One of the people in a group to which you belong tells racist and sexist jokes. You find the jokes very offensive, but you don't want to create tension in the group or make the person who tells the jokes feel bad. You just want the jokes to stop.

Aggressive response:

Assertive response:

Deferential response

Name _____

Activity 8.7: Distinguishing Between Love and Commitment (With InfoTrac-College Edition)

Purposes: To increase your understanding of the difference between love and commitment; To provide concrete experience in identifying language that reflects love and commitment.

Instructions

1.   If you do not remember the textbook's discussion of differences between love and commitment, reread *Elements of Satisfying Personal Relationships.*

2.   Listed below are 10 statements that friends and romantic partners might make to each other. In the blank to the left of each statement indicate whether the statement expresses commitment (C) or love (L).

3.   Answers appear at the end of the chapter.

_____   1.   I have a really great time with you.

_____   2.   Talking with you is so helpful in sorting out my feelings.

_____   3.   I like to think about how we'll be 10 or 15 years from now.

_____   4.   I feel great when I'm with you.

_____   5.   I intend to be faithful to you all of my life.

_____   6.   I've never felt this way about anyone else before.

_____   7.   I'm crazy about you, but if you don't learn to control your temper, our relationship is over.

_____   8.   Our relationship would be so much more enjoyable if you didn't have these outbursts of temper.

_____   9.   I feel so close to you right now.

_____   10.   Nothing will ever come between us.

Search *InfoTrac-College Edition* keywords "love and commitment" to see how articles distinguish between love and commitment. Bring ideas from these articles to share with the rest of your class.

Name _____

Activity 8.8: Rating the Supportiveness of Communication Climates

Purposes: To provide you with experience in identifying communication that tends to foster defensive and supportive climates between people; To demonstrate the practical value of knowledge about supportive and defense-producing styles of communicating.

Instructions

1. If you do not have a clear memory of the kinds of communication that cultivate defensive and supportive communication climates, reread *Defensive and Supportive Climates* in your textbook.

2. Identify two personal relationships that you can observe. One relationship should have a supportive climate in which partners seem to feel safe, at ease, and supported by each other. The second relationship should be one in which a defensive climate prevails. Partners should seem to feel on guard and unsure of each other's motives and support. You may wish to select relationships between characters in television programs or films so that your observations do not interfere with the relationships.

3. Use form A below to identify examples of communication that is linked to defensive and supportive climates in the relationship that has a supportive climate. Try to record each example of supportive and defense-producing communication.

4. Use form B below to identify examples of communication that is linked to defensive and supportive climates in the relationship that has a defensive climate. Try to record each example of supportive and defense-producing communication.

5. Compare the profiles of communication for the two relationships.

FORM A:

**USE TO CODE COMMUNICATION IN A RELATIONSHIP
THAT HAS A SUPPORTIVE CLIMATE**

Communication Type	Number of Instances Observed
Evaluation	
Description	
Certainty	
Provisionalism	
Strategy	
Spontaneity	
Control-orientation	
Problem-orientation	
Neutrality	
Empathy	
Superiority	
Equality	

Name _____

Activity 8.8: Rating the Supportiveness of Communication Climates

<u>Purposes</u>: To provide you with experience in identifying communication that tends to foster defensive and supportive climates between people; To demonstrate the practical value of knowledge about supportive and defense-producing styles of communicating.

<u>Instructions</u>

1.   If you do not have a clear memory of the kinds of communication that cultivate defensive and supportive communication climates, reread *Defensive and Supportive Climates* in your textbook.

2.   Identify two personal relationships that you can observe. One relationship should have a supportive climate in which partners seem to feel safe, at ease, and supported by each other. The second relationship should be one in which a defensive climate prevails. Partners should seem to feel on guard and unsure of each other's motives and support. You may wish to select relationships between characters in television programs or films so that your observations do not interfere with the relationships.

3.   Use form A below to identify examples of communication that is linked to defensive and supportive climates in the relationship that has a supportive climate. Try to record each example of supportive and defense-producing communication.

4.   Use form B below to identify examples of communication that is linked to defensive and supportive climates in the relationship that has a defensive climate. Try to record each example of supportive and defense-producing communication.

5.   Compare the profiles of communication for the two relationships.

FORM A:

**USE TO CODE COMMUNICATION IN A RELATIONSHIP
THAT HAS A SUPPORTIVE CLIMATE**

Communication Type	Number of Instances Observed
Evaluation	
Description	
Certainty	
Provisionalism	
Strategy	
Spontaneity	
Control-orientation	
Problem-orientation	
Neutrality	
Empathy	
Superiority	
Equality	

FORM B:

USE TO CODE COMMUNICATION IN A RELATIONSHIP
THAT HAS A DEFENSIVE CLIMATE

Communication Type	Number of Instances Observed
Evaluation	
Description	
Certainty	
Provisionalism	
Strategy	
Spontaneity	
Control-orientation	
Problem-orientation	
Neutrality	
Empathy	
Superiority	
Equality	

Name _____

Activity 8.9: Recognizing Relational Dialectics

<u>Purpose</u>: To give you experience in identifying relational dialectics in everyday situations.

<u>Instructions</u>: If you do not recall the textbook's discussion of relational dialectics, reread *Comfort with Relational Dialectics*. Listed below are six descriptions of common dynamics in personal relationships. Identify which relational dialectic is most prominent in each. Record your answers in the blanks to the left of the descriptions. Answers appear at the end of the chapter.

Relational Dialectic

<u>Example</u>

novelty/predictability

Description of Dynamics

Erin and Mike want to take a vacation and are undecided whether to return to a place they know and like or to go somewhere new and different.

_____

1. Jennie wants to tell her friend Anne about her problems with school, but Jennie also wants to keep her academic difficulties private.

_____

2. Tyronne and David have gotten together to watch football games every weekend for 2 years. They really enjoy this pattern in their friendship, yet they are also feeling it's getting stale.

_____

3. Marilyn likes the fact that her boyfriend Jim respects her right not to tell him about certain aspects of her life. At the same time, she sometimes feels that what they don't know abo each other creates a barrier between them.

Relational Dialectic	Description of Dynamics
Example	
novelty/predictability	Erin and Mike want to take a vacation and are undecided whether to return to a place they know and like or to go somewhere new and different.
	4. Robert feels that he and Navita would be closer if they did more things together, yet he also likes the fact that each of them has independent interests.
	5. Danny feels he and Kate have fallen into routines in how they spend time together. On one hand, he likes the steady rhythm they have; on the other hand, it seems boring.
	6. After spending a week together on a backpacking trip, Mike and Ed get back to campus and don't call or see each other for several days.

Name _____

Activity 8.10: Communicating Levels of Confirmation

Purpose: To give you practice in creating communication that expresses different levels of confirmation of another person.

Instructions: If you do not recall the three levels of confirmation and the communication that creates them, reread *Levels of Confirmation and Disconfirmation*. Listed below are four situations. For each one, write a statement that expresses each of the three levels of confirmation: recognition, acknowledgment, and endorsement. Use parentheses to indicate nonverbal communication of each level of confirmation.

Example

A two year old child runs up to you and says, "Look, look, I found a four leaf clover."

A.   recognition: Hello. (Smile)

B.   acknowledgement: So you're pretty excited, aren't you?

C.   endorsement: Wow! You're right. You did find a four leaf clover.

1.   Your best friend comes to your place without having mentioned she/he was coming by. Your friend walks in and says, "I'm really worried about what's happening between my parents. They seem angry with each other all the time lately, and I think they may be thinking about a separation or divorce."

A.   recognition:

B.   acknowledgment:

C.   endorsement

2. At a meeting of a political group, someone you know only casually says to you, "All we ever do in this group is talk. We never really DO anything. I am very frustrated by the lack of action."

    A.   recognition:

    B.   acknowledgment:

    C.   endorsement:

3. While you are home over break, one of your parents says to you, "I'm worried about your uncle. His health is failing, and I think maybe we need to move him into a nursing home."

    A.   recognition:

    B.   acknowledgment:

    C.   endorsement:

4. The person whom you have been dating steadily for 4 months tells you, "I don't like the way we handle conflict. Whenever we disagree about something, it seems that each of us digs our heels in and refuses to listen to the other or to even try to understand the other's point of view."

    A.   recognition:

    B.   acknowledgment:

    C.   endorsement:

Name _____

Activity 8.11: Assertiveness Inventory
(Using the WWW)

Purpose: To assess your general level of assertiveness and determine ways you can become more assertive.

Instructions: Visit the web site (http://discoveryhealth.queendom.com/access_assertiveness.html) to take an on-line survey that tests your general level of assertiveness. After responding to the questions, write your score out of 100 and what that score means (see web site for details). Next, visit the web site http://www.tsuccess.dircon.co.uk/assertivenesstraining.htm and make a list of the points that you can apply to your own communication practices to become more assertive.

My Score _____ (out of 100) which indicates that _____

_____

Points I Can Apply to Become More Assertive

1. _____

2. _____

3. _____

4. _____

5. _____

Answers to Distinguishing Between Love and Commitment

1. One, two, four, six, seven, nine, and ten are statements of love. Each expresses a feeling and/or refers to the present time.

2. Three, five, and eight are statements of commitment. Each expresses an intention or assumption that the relationship will continue.

3. Note especially the difference between statements 8 and 9. In statement 8, the continuity of the relationship is contingent on the partner's learning to control her or his temper. In statement 9, the continuity of the relationship is assumed and only the level of enjoyment it affords is uncertain.

Answers to Recognizing Relational Dialectics

1. openness/closedness	4. autonomy/connection
2. novelty/predictability	5. novelty/predictability
3. openness/closedness	6. autonomy/connection

Using Your Everyday Encounters Premium Website

Use your *Everyday Encounters* premium website for quick access to the electronic study resources that accompany this text. The *Everyday Encounters* web site offers an interactive version of many of the activities in this chapter. You can complete these activities online and submit them electronically to your instructor. All of the web links included in this chapter as well as in the accompanying main text chapter are maintained on the web site, accessible through http://www.thomsonedu.com.

Included on the website is access to the Continuing the Conversation video scenario and questions featured in this chapter. Watch, listen to, and analyze the Continuing the Conversation case featuring *Alan O'Connor: Manager* included at the end of Chapter 8 in your main text. The full transcript of the *Alan O'Connor: Manager* conversation is included in your textbook. Watch, listen to and critique the conversation by completing the Conversation Analysis. You can compare your response to the authors by clicking on the Submit button at the end of the form.

Websites of Interest

The following URLs are maintained and updated on the *Everyday Encounters* web site, accessible through http://www.thomsonedu.com. We recommend you begin your web searches at this site to ensure that the links listed below are still active.

Name: Assertiveness Skills
Developer: Dr. Tom Stevens
Brief Description: This web page explains how to create harmonious relationships and intimacy through empathic listening and being assertive.
URL: http://www.csulb.edu/~tstevens

Name: Organizational Climate Survey Sample Report
Developer: Management Development Systems
Brief Description: This web page provides a sample organizational climate survey.
URL: http://www.mds-mss.com/Organizational_Climate_Survey.html

Name: Life @ Lucent
Developer: Lucent Technologies
Brief Description: A description of the culture and work climate at Lucent Technologies.
URL: http://www.lucent.com/work/culture.html

Name: Cisco Systems Culture
Developer: Cisco Systems
Brief Description: A description of the culture and work climate at Cisco Systems.
URL: http://www.cisco.com/jobs/us/culture.shtml

Name: Blue Mountain
Developer: Blue Mountain.com
Brief Description: This web site allows users to send free electronic greeting cards to anyone with an e-mail address. Consider this site in relation to how eCards can be used in the cultivation of communication climates.
URL: http://www.bluemountain.com

Name: Ethnocentrism
Developer: Wikipedia
Brief Description: Defines and give examples of ethnocentrism. Also includes links to related articles on ethnocentrism.
URL: http://en.wikipedia.org/wiki/Ethnocentrism

Name: Johari Window: The Psychodynamics of Leadership and Influence
Developer: David M. Boje, New Mexico State U
Brief Description: Links the Johari Window with leadership. Explains the results of the Johari Window Questionnaire in terms of leadership and influence tendencies. Click on STUFF, then JoHari Window
URL: http://cbae.nmsu.edu/~dboje

Self Test

Multiple Choice

_____ 1.   _____ is a decision to remain with a relationship.

    A.   Commitment
    B.   Trust
    C.   Ethnocentrism
    D.   Investment

_____ 2.   Reciprocity of self-disclosures is especially important:

    A.   in the early stages of relationship development
    B.   after trust has been established between partners
    C.   in stable and enduring relationship
    D.   in intercultural relationships.

_____ 3.   _____ refers to what we contribute to a relationship that we could not get back if the relationship ended.

A.   Commitment
B.   Trust
C.   Ethnocentrism
D.   Investment

4.   "I accept and agree with your feelings." This statement is an example of which level of confirming communication?

A.   recognition
B.   acknowledgment
C.   endorsement
D.   empathy

5.   "Your paper is poorly organized." This statement is an example of which kind of defensive-producing communication?

A.   evaluation
B.   strategy
C.   provisionalism
D.   problem orientation

6.   When you use assertive communication, you:

A.   put your needs ahead of others' needs.
B.   subordinate your needs to others' needs.
C.   state your feelings or needs clearly without disparaging others' feelings or needs.
D.   ignore others' feelings and needs to be sure that yours are met.

7.   The most central and continuous tension in most close relationships is a result of which of the following dialectical tensions?

A.   closedness/openness
B.   novelty/predictability
C.   autonomy/connection
D.   stability/change

True/False

_____ 8. Self-disclosure is a key gauge of closeness.

_____ 9. When communicating with persons with disabilities, it's best to talk to the companion or interpreter.

_____ 10. Even positive evaluations can foster defensiveness between people.

_____ 11. The most basic requirement for healthy communication is confirmation.

_____ 12. Neutralization is one an effective method of handling conflict of opposing needs because both parties are fully satisfied when using this strategy.

Essay

13. Identify and describe one relationship in which you primarily experience closeness in the doing and one relationship in which you primarily experience closeness in dialogue.

14. Compare and contrast the communication in one of your satisfying and one of your unsatisfying personal relationships. Be sure to use the four elements of personal relationships discussed in the chapter.

15. Evaluate the climate in a work environment in terms of Gibbs' aspects of confirming and disconfirming communication behaviors.

Personal Reflections

1. Identify one relationship in which you feel on-guard and defensive and one relationship in which you feel comfortable and supported. Describe and analyze the communication behaviors in each relationship. To what extent do the defensive and supportive communication behaviors discussed in the text explain the climates of these two relationships?

2. Pick a situation in which someone with whom you are talking seems defensive. Consciously engage in supportive communication behaviors and avoid ones likely to produce defensiveness. Analyze what happens in terms of the other person's comfort and communication.

3. In terms of the Johari Window, one way for information to move from the hidden window to the open window is through self-disclosure. However, information can also move from the hidden window to the open window by "outing" someone. With "outing," another person discloses information they know about a person to others. Describe a situation where you have been "outed," where you have "outed" anyone, or where you have heard of someone being "outed"? How might it feel to be outed? Reflect on whether "outing" is an ethical form of communication.

Chapter 9:   Managing Conflict in Relationships

I.   <u>Conflict</u> exists when individuals who depend upon each other express different views, interest, or goals, and perceive them as incompatible or oppositional.

    A.   Conflict must be recognized and/or expressed. I often express conflict verbally by saying

        _____;

        I often express conflict nonverbally by _____

        _____

    B.   All parties involved in the conflict must depend upon each other.

    C.   Conflict arises when we perceive that there are incompatible goals, preferences, or decisions that must be resolved to maintain the relationship.

II.   There are basic principles of conflict.

    A.   Conflict is a natural part of our relationships that indicates the people involved are connected to each other.

    B.   Conflict may be open, explicit, or overt, or it may be hidden, implicit, or covert. An example of overt conflict in my life is _____

        1.   <u>Passive aggression</u>, a common form of covert conflict, occurs when individuals act aggressively, but deny the aggressive behavior. An example of covert conflict in my life is _____

2.   Covert conflict often happens through <u>games</u> in which real conflicts are hidden or denied.

C.   Our responses to conflict can benefit or harm ourselves and the relationship in which we are involved. An example of a time when conflict benefited one of my relationships is

_____ ;

An example of a time when conflict harmed one of my relationships is

_____

III.   Social influences (cultural background, gender, and sexual orientation) affect our orientation toward and responses to conflict.

IV.   How conflicts are managed directly influences the future of the relationship.

V.   Handling conflict in constructive ways can promote personal and relational growth.

VI.   There are three basic orientations people have toward conflict.

A.   A <u>lose-lose approach</u> assumes that expressing conflict is unhealthy for everyone involved in the relationship. This approach works well when we are trying to figure out if we need to engage in conflict, especially if the issue is less important than others. An example of a lose-lose orientation that I have seen is _____

_____

B.   A <u>win-lose approach</u> assumes that expressing conflict leads to one person benefiting and the other person not achieving a desired outcome. This approach works well when we have low commitment to the relationship and/or a small desire to exert the energy necessary to engage in conflict. An example of a win-lose orientation that I have seen is

_____

C.   A <u>win-win approach</u> assumes that expressing conflict leads to all people involved working together to come up with a solution that is acceptable to everyone. An example of a win-win orientation that I have seen is _____

_____

VII.   Most people have relatively consistent patterns they employ to respond to conflict.

A.   We use <u>exit responses</u> when we leave the relationship, either physically or psychologically. Exit responses are most consistent with _____ orientations.

B.   We use <u>neglect responses</u> when we minimize or deny the conflict exists. Neglect responses are most consistent with _____ and _____ orientations.

C.   We use <u>loyalty responses</u> when we remain committed to continuing the relationship and choose to put up with the differences. Loyalty responses are most consistent with _____ orientations.

D.   We use <u>voice responses</u> when we actively seek to talk openly about and resolve the conflict. Voice responses are most consistent with _____ orientations.

VIII.   The communication pattern we choose during conflict can help or hinder the relationship.

A.   Ineffective communication damages efforts to resolve the conflict, harms individuals, and jeopardizes relational health.

1.	Early in the process, we use communication that disconfirms the other person.

2.	Once a negative climate has been established, we maintain it by engaging in additional negative communication (e.g., frequent interruptions).

3.	In the later stages of the conflict, all parties feel the pressure to resolve the conflict, usually on their own terms rather than taking the other person's proposals into account.

B.	Constructive communication is open, nonjudgmental, confirming, and non-strategic.

1.	Prior to the conflict, people confirm each other by recognizing and acknowledging each other's concerns and feelings; when the conflict arises, they know that they are both working together to come up with a solution.

2.	In the middle stages, everyone focus on the specific issues at hand and eliminates all potential distractions, including previous conflicts.

3.	In the final resolution stages, both partners work to take parts of each proposal put on the table to agree upon a solution everyone can accept.

IX.	Several skills are identified that are essential for effective conflict management: attending to the relationship level of meaning; communicating supportively; listening mindfully; taking responsibility for your thoughts, feelings, and issues; checking perceptions; looking for points of agreement; looking for ways to preserve the other person's face; and imagining how you will feel in the future.

X.	There are at least five guidelines for improving conflict communication.

A. We need to focus on the entire system in which communication occurs rather than just on the conflict or disagreement. An example of a time when I should have considered the whole system is _____

_____

B. We need to pay attention to the timing of conflicts: chronemics (make sure all parties are completely present mentally; be flexible about when to handle conflict; and set aside tangential issues for another time). An example of a time when I should have paid more attention to timing is _____

_____

C. If we care about the other person and our relationship, we should aim for a win-win approach. An example of a time when I should have striven for a win-win resolution is

_____

D. Honor and respect yourself as well as the other person/people involved and the relationship. An example of a time when I should have honored and respected everyone involved in the conflict is _____

_____

E. Consider whether it is appropriate to put aside our own needs if there is no rule or standard that says we should grant the other compassion. An example of a time when I should have exhibited grace is _____

_____

Additional Vocabulary

For each of the terms listed below, generate a personal example that illustrates the concept.

Bracketing _____

_____

Contracting _____

_____

Cross-complaining _____

_____

Games _____

_____

Kitchensinking _____

_____

Grace _____

Key Concepts

bracketing
contracting
exit response
games
grace
interpersonal conflict
kitchensinking
letting go

lose-lose
loyalty response
neglect response
passive aggression
voice response
win-lose
win-win

Activities

Title	Individual	Partner	Group	Ethno.	Internet/InfoTrac
9.1 Identifying Your Style(s) of Responding to Conflict	✓				
9.2 Generating Different Responses to Conflict	✓				
9.3 Identifying Orientations to Conflict	✓				✓
9.4 Understanding Your Conflict Script	✓				
9.5 Managing Conflict	✓				✓

Name _____

Activity 9.1: Identifying Your Style(s) of Responding to Conflict

Purpose: To provide you with feedback on your preferred responses to interpersonal conflict.

Instructions: Read the scenarios below. For each one, circle which of the four possible responses you think it is most likely you would follow. To score your conflict response inventory, follow the instructions at the end of this inventory.

1.   The person that you have been dating for 6 months tells you she/he is upset by your lack of interest in spending time with her/his friends. You don't want to spend time with your partner's friends, but she/he sees this as an issue that the two of you need to resolve. In this situation, you would be most likely to:

   A.   Walk out on the conversation.
   B.   Tell her/him that the issue isn't important.
   C.   Say nothing and hope the issue will go away.
   D.   Actively work to find a resolution that satisfies both of you.

2.   Last week a friend let you use his/her computer when yours crashed. Accidentally, you erased a couple of files on your friend's computer. Later, the friend confronts you about the erased files and the friend seems really angry. In this situation, you would be most likely to:

   A.   Tune out your friend's criticism and anger.
   B.   Agree that you had made an error and ask how you could make it up to your friend.
   C.   Say nothing and hope your friend's anger blows over and the friendship continues.
   D.   Tell your friend that it's not a big deal since he/she always backs up the hard drive.

3.   Your roommate tells you that you are a slob and that she/he wants the two of you to agree to some ground rules about cleaning and putting things up. In this situation, you would be most likely to:

   A.   Agree to be more neat, even though you don't think it's fair that you should have to operate by your roommate's standards.
   B.   Tell your roommate that cleaning is not a big deal in the big picture of living together.
   C.   Agree that the two of you differ in how you like the place to look and offer to work out some mutually acceptable rules.
   D.   Leave the situation and hope that your roommate will let the matter drop.

4. The person you have been dating for a while says that you are too critical and too negative, and she/he says she/he wants you to work on changing that aspect of your behavior. Although you realize this may be a fair criticism of you, you find it uncomfortable to hear. Further, you have no idea how you could eliminate or improve your tendency to be judgmental. In this situation, you would be most likely to

    A. Agree with your dating partner's perceptions and ask if she/he has any suggestions for how you might reduce your critical, negative tendencies.
    B. Shrug and ignore the criticism.
    C. Say nothing and hope things get better.
    D. Point out that being critical is not really a major issue in whether two people are compatible.

5. Your parents call you to criticize you for not staying in touch. They say they want you to come home more often and call a couple of times each week. You are very involved in the campus scene and don't want to be running home all the time. In this situation, you would be most likely to

    A. Tell your parents they are creating a problem when none really exists
    B. Agree that you haven't stayed in touch and promise to be better in the future; then follow through on your promise even though it isn't your preference.
    C. Tell your parents that you want to work with them to come up with ways you can stay in better touch without separating you from the campus too much.
    D. Hang up the phone and not return their calls in the future.

Scoring the Conflict Response Inventory

The four choices for your action in each scenario represent the responses of exit, voice, loyalty, and neglect. If you do not recall what these responses are, review *Responses to Conflict* in the textbook.

Scoring:

	Exit	Voice	Loyalty	Neglect
1.	A	D	C	B
2.	A	B	C	D
3.	D	C	A	B
4.	B	A	C	D
5.	D	C	B	A

Questions to consider in interpreting your scores:

1.   Did you rely on a single response in 3 or more of the situations?

2.   Did you rely more on exit and neglect (combined) than on voice and loyalty (combined)?

3.   What are the advantages and disadvantages of your response style(s)?

Name _____

Activity 9.2: Generating Different Responses to Conflict

Purposes: To give you practice in generating communication that reflects each of the four responses to interpersonal conflict; To increase your repertoire of methods for responding to interpersonal conflict.

Instructions

1.   If you do not recall the textbook's discussion of different responses to conflict, review *Responses to Conflict*.

2.   Listed below are 5 conflict scenarios. For each one, write 4 responses--one each that reflects exit, voice, loyalty, and neglect responses.

Scenario 1

The person you have been dating suggests that it's time the two of you talked about commitment. You feel unready to discuss a serious relationship, but your partner insists that she/he thinks the two of you need to talk about it.

A.   exit response:

B.   voice response:

C.   loyalty response:

D.   neglect response:

Scenario 2

One of your friends brings up a political race, and you make a comment about the strengths of the candidate you support. Your friend says, "I can't believe you support that jerk. What has he done for the environment?"

A.   exit response:

B.   voice response:

C.   loyalty response:

D.   neglect response:

Scenario 3

One of your co-workers continuously misses deadlines in turning in reports to you. Since your reports require information from the co-worker's reports, your reports also are late. You don't want your late reports to interfere with your raises and advancement. You'd like for the co-worker to be more prompt.

A.   exit response:

B.   voice response:

C.   loyalty response:

D.   neglect response:

Scenario 4

You tell your parents you'd like to take a term off from school. They are strongly opposed to the idea and they tell you to stay in school.

A.   exit response:

B.   voice response:

C.   loyalty response:

D.   neglect response:

Scenario 5

You and your friend generally get together to watch the play-offs at his apartment. This year, your friend suggests that the two of you go downtown to one of the bars that has a giant screen. Where you watch doesn't really matter to you.

A.   exit response:

B.   voice response:

C.   loyalty response:

D.   neglect response:

Name _____

Activity 9.3: Identifying Orientations to Conflict (With InfoTrac-College Edition)

Purpose: To give you practice in recognizing orientations to conflict in concrete situations.

Instructions: For each of the statements listed below, indicate which orientation to conflict it most clearly reflects. Use the letters below to indicate the corresponding orientations to conflict. Correct answers appear at the end of the chapter.

A.   win-lose

B.   lose-lose

C.   win-win

_____   1.   We can't both be satisfied with a resolution to this problem.

_____   2.   Since we disagree on where to go for our vacation, let's just not go anywhere.

_____   3.   We are never going to see eye to eye on this. I think my preference should prevail.

_____   4.   I think if we keep talking, we will figure out something that both of us can live with.

_____   5.   I can't stand fighting. Everyone loses.

_____   6.   No matter what you say, I'm not giving any ground on this issue. I feel very strongly and I expect you to go along with me this time.

_____   7.   There's no point in arguing about money. All we ever do is hurt each other without solving anything.

_____   8.   I'm willing to go along with your preference on the model of car if you'll go along with my preference for color and added features.

_____   9.   Look: There are only two possibilities in this situation, so both of us can't get what we want.

_____   10.   I wonder if there aren't some solutions other that the two we have come up with so far. I think if we keep talking, we might be able to come up with something workable for both of us.

Search *InfoTrac-College Edition* keywords "win-win" to find articles that discuss win-win approaches to conflict management. Bring ideas from these articles to share with the rest of your class.

Name _____

Activity 9.4: Understanding Your Conflict Script

<u>Purposes</u>: To help you recognize ways in which your family shaped your views of conflict. To invite you to reconsider any unproductive conflict scripts that you learned.

<u>Instructions</u>

1.   Respond to the questions below.

2.   To summarize your responses to the questions, create a written description of the conflict script you learned in your family.

3.   Identify any aspects of your conflict script that you would like to change.

4.   Indicate strategies you will follow for revising aspects of your conflict script that you do not want to retain.

Did you ever witness your parents engaging in conflict?

If so, how often did they adopt win-win, win-lose, and lose-lose orientations toward conflict?

How often did each of your (step)parents rely on exit, voice, loyalty, and neglect responses to conflict?

A.   Father

B.   Mother

C.   Stepfather

D.   Stepmother

Do you recall any explicit statements about conflict that your parents made? For example, some parents tell children "conflict is bad" or "conflict is healthy." What do you recall hearing from your (step)parents?

What happened when conflict occurred in your family?

    A.   Did individuals demonstrate respect for one another and one another's views?

    B.   Was there any residual anger or negative feeling following conflicts?

    C.   Did your parents try to get others to take sides?

Write the conflict script that you were taught in your family:

Identify any aspects of the conflict script that you learned in your family that you would like to revise or eliminate from your own views of conflict. For each aspect of your conflict script that you would like to revise, indicate 2 specific strategies you might follow to create the desired change.

Desired Change in Script	Strategies for Changing
Example	
I want to change what I learned about trying to win in every case.	a. I will monitor my inclination to try to win just for the sake of winning.
	b. I will paraphrase other people's views to encourage myself to consider what they think and feel.
1.	a.
	b.
2.	a.
	b.
3.	a.
	b.

Name _____

Activity 9.5: Managing Conflict
(With InfoTrac-College Edition and Using the WWW)

<u>Purpose</u>: To research the most recent trends and approaches towards managing conflict.

<u>Instructions</u>: Use your *InfoTrac-College Edition* and a web search engine (such as AltaVista or Google) to locate recent articles and web pages on conflict management in the workplace. Make a list of at three articles and/or web pages. What are the latest trends in how researchers and practitioners approach conflict management? What guidelines are provided for how to manage conflict successfully?

Article/Web Page #1:

Article/Web Page #2:

Article/Web Page #3:

Answers to the Conflict Orientations Instrument

1.   A

2.   B

3.   A

4.   C

5.   B

6.   A

7.   B

8.   C

9.   A

10.   C

Using Your Everyday Encounters Premium Website

Use your *Everyday Encounters* premium website for quick access to the electronic study resources that accompany this text. The *Everyday Encounters* web site offers an interactive version of many of the activities in this chapter. You can complete these activities online and submit them electronically to your instructor. All of the web links included in this chapter as well as in the accompanying main text chapter are maintained on the web site, accessible through http://www.thomsonedu.com.

Included on the website is access to the Continuing the Conversation video scenario and questions featured in this chapter. Watch, listen to, and analyze the Continuing the Conversation case featuring *Jan and Ken* included at the end of Chapter 9 in your main text. The full transcript of Jan and Ken's conversation is included in your textbook. Watch, listen to and critique the conversation by completing the Conversation Analysis. You can compare your response to the authors by clicking on the Submit button at the end of the form.

Websites of Interest

The following URLs are maintained and updated on the *Everyday Encounters* web site, accessible through http://www.thomsonedu.com. We recommend you begin your web searches at this site to ensure that the links listed below are still active.

Name: Addressing Interpersonal Conflict
Developer: Carter McNamara, MBA, PhD, and the Management Assistance Program
Brief Description: An index of online resources related to interpersonal conflict in the workplace.
URL: http://www.mapnp.org/library/intrpsnl/conflict.htm

Name: Interpersonal Conflict Management for Police
Developer: The Consortium for Research on Emotional Intelligence in Organizations
Brief Description: Describes a program for training police officers to more effectively intervene in interpersonal conflicts in the course of their work.
URL: http://www.eiconsortium.org/model_programs/interpersonal_conflict_training_police.htm

Name: Dealing with Worldviews in Interpersonal Conflict
Developer: Anne Giacalone DiDomenico
Brief Description: On the CADRE (The National Center on Dispute Resolution) website, this article examines the ways in which individual and collective worldviews influence conflict situations.
URL: http://www.directionservice.org/cadre/worldviews.cfm

Name: Forgiveness Institute
Developer: University of Wisconsin-Madison

Brief Description: This website is dedicated to helping people gain knowledge about forgiveness and to use that knowledge for personal, group, and societal renewal.
URL: http://www.forgiveness-institute.org

Name: A Short Divorce Course
Developer: Ed Sherman, Attorney and Nolo Press
Brief Description: This portion of the Divorce Helpline website offers a short course on how to make the process of divorce go more smoothly, reduce conflict, and keep parties out of court.
URL: http://www.divorcehelp.com/shortcourse/shortcourse.html

Name: Violence, Aggression and Passive-Aggression in the Workplace Remedies
Developer: Rudy Nydegger, Graduate Management Institute at Union College
Brief Description: In this research article, the author defines and discusses how to handle violent and aggressive behavior in the workplace.
URL: http://www.esc.edu/ESConline/across_esc/forumjournal.nsf/web+view/
29B0B2D84F5B2CA7852569E5000B6DE7?opendocument

Self Test

Multiple Choice

_____ 1. Ed is angry at his friend Bob because Bob damaged a CD Ed lent him. Instead of telling Bob he is angry, Ed deliberately plays music that Bob dislikes when Bob comes over to visit. This is an example of:

    A. win-win orientation
    B. overt conflict
    C. kitchensinking
    D. covert conflict

_____ 2. "I'll do anything to avoid conflict. I think when people have conflict, everybody gets hurt and nothing is solved." This statement reflects which of the following views of conflict?

    A. lose-lose
    B. win-lose
    C. win-win
    D. voice

_____ 3. "If there is a conflict, I want to be the one who prevails, not the one who has to cave in. Those are the only two positions when people disagree." This statement reflects which of the following views of conflict?

    A.   lose-lose
    B.   win-lose
    C.   win-win
    D.   voice

_____ 4. The ____ response to conflict may be an effective strategy when the partners need time to cool off.

    A.   loyalty
    B.   exit
    C.   neglect
    D.   voice

_____ 5. In response to your complaint that you have two presentations and a group assignment next week, your partner replies: "That's nothing compared to my two tests and three papers—plus I work 20 hours next week." This is an example of _____ in covert conflict.

    A.   a game
    B.   kitchensinking
    C.   dual perspective
    D.   shunning

_____ 6. Brenda and Zachary are engaged in conflict. The discussion begins with Brenda's state that she is not satisfied with how they spend their money. Zachary responds by talking about his anger at the amount of time Brenda spends at work. She then brings up her frustration with his lack of involvement in cooking and cleaning. He reminds her that she tries to avoid visits with his family. This description suggests that Zachary and Brenda are involved in:

    A.   self-summarizing
    B.   cross-complaining
    C.   kitchensinking
    D.   metacommunication

True/False

_____ 7. Productive conflict communication includes counter proposals.

_____ 8. Americans perceive conflict differently than persons of other cultures.

_____ 9. In conflict individuals must be interdependent.

_____ 10. Conflict is not an inevitable part of all relationships if the partners establish a positive climate.

_____ 11. In general, women tend to avoid confronting conflict more than men.

_____ 12. Effective communication during conflict includes dealing immediately with an issue regardless of the time.

Essay

13. Discuss different orientations to conflict based on culture and social communities (including gender, sexual orientation, and race/ethnicity).

14. Distinguish between counterproposals and contracting. Your answer should include specific examples and illustrations.

15. Describe and explain the concept of grace. Your response should define the term, explain what it does and does not include, and indicate when grace likely to be is appropriate and inadvisable.

Personal Reflections

1. Analyze your responses to conflict in terms of the exit-voice-loyalty-neglect model discussed in the text. How often do you use each response style in your friendships and romantic relationships? Which style do you use least? What are the results of the way(s) you respond to conflict?

2. Describe a situation in which you had a conflict with a close friend or romantic partner and you managed to work it out constructively. Analyze what happened by discussing how your behavior and your partner's followed or violated principles for effective conflict discussed in the text.

3. Consider how you deal with conflict in relationships with people at work. Is it similar to how you handle conflict in non-work relationships (or in non-work contexts if you are also a friend/intimate with someone you work with)? In addition to noting any similarities or differences, consider explanations for each.

Chapter 10:   Friendships in Our Lives

I.   Friendships are an important relationship in our lives; they are unique because there are no rules, laws, or institutional structures that create and maintain them.

     A.   We expect to invest time, energy, thoughts, and feelings into our friendships.

     B.   We expect to develop an emotional closeness that includes self disclosure.

          1.   Some people, particularly feminine women and androgynous men, express intimacy through dialogue. An example of expressing intimacy through dialogue is _____

          _____

          2.   Some people, particularly masculine men, express intimacy through shared activities. An example of expressing intimacy through activities is _____

          _____

     C.   We expect that our friends accept both the positive and negative aspects of our selves; we do not feel we need to hide thoughts or feelings from our friends.

     D.   We expect to develop a level of trust, both confidence in the fact that friends will do what they say they will do and in the belief that a friend cares about us and our welfare.

     E.   We expect friends to indicate their support for us by showing, either verbally through dialogue or nonverbally through action, that they care.

F.   Although our personal experience, gender, and ethnic background influence how we experience and express friendship, there is much common ground about what people expect and value in friendships. Examples of what I expect and value in my friendships include _____ _____

_____ ____

II.   Friendships tend to follow relatively stable rules for how they develop and function.

     A.   The majority of friendships work through a set of stages.

          1.   Friendships begin with an initial encounter, either planned or accidental.

          2.   Friendly relations occur when we spend time checking out whether we could develop a more lasting relationship with this person. I usually check out _____

               when considering a new friend.

          3.   In the third stage, we work toward creating a longer-term friendship by starting to disclose our feelings, attitudes, values, thoughts, and interests. At this point, I usually disclose _____ about myself.

          4.   Nascent friendship is when we begin to think of ourselves as friends and to work out our own rules for the relationship. _____

               is a rule in my friendship with _____

5.   When we are in the stabilized friendship stage, we have determined that this relationship will continue, take future encounters for granted, and work at creating a high level of trust.

6.   When one or both people stop investing in the relationship, get pulled in different directions by family or career demands, or violate trust or a rule, the friendship can begin to wane; communication tends to become defensive if it exists at all. One reason one of my friendships waned or deteriorated is because_____

_____

B.   <u>Relationships rules</u>, even though we often are not consciously aware of them, help us figure out what is appropriate and inappropriate in this friendship. An example of a relationship rule that exists in all of my friendships is _____

_____

III.   Like all relationships, there are various things that make them difficult to develop and maintain.

A.   <u>Internal tensions</u> are relationship stressors that grow out of the individuals involved in the relationship.

1.   Relational dialectics (autonomy/connection, openness/privacy, and novelty/familiarity) create tension when the people involved in the friendship have different expectations and/or needs. An example of a time when relational dialectics created tension in one of my friendships is _____

_____

2.   Social diversity creates tension when our interpretation of different communication styles or perceptions create misunderstandings. An example of a

time when I saw social diversity create tension in a friendship is _____

_____

3.   Sexual attraction creates tension when two friends have agreed not to add romance to their relationship or if one person wants romance and the other does not. An example of a time when I saw sexual attraction create tension in a friendship is

_____

B.   External tensions are relationship stressors that grow out of the situation or context surrounding the relationship.

1.   Because our lives are complex and friendships have no rules governing how often, when, and where we interact, they are frequently the easiest relationship to neglect when we have too much to do. An example of a time when I had to meet too many demands to give a friendship the time it deserved is_____

_____

2.   Our friendships change as we make changes in our lives (e.g., starting a new educational stage, a new career, a family; caring for others). An example of a change that affect a friendship of mine is _____

3.   Geographic distance is becoming a larger constraint as we become a more mobile society. An example of a friendship that was affected by geographic distance is _

_____

IV.   In addition to the general principles discussed in earlier chapters, there are four specific guidelines for enhancing communication in friendships.

A.	We need to engage in dual perspective so that we can see the friendship as our friend does as well as understand the thoughts and feelings this person expresses. An example of a friendship in which I should have engaged (more) in dual perspective is _____

_____

B.	We need to communicate honestly, even when that is not what the other person wants to hear or it does not paint a positive picture. An example of a time when I should have communicated honestly is _____

_____

C.	We need to be open to difference and recognize that every friendship or situation does not come in a neat either-or package. An example of a time when I should have been open to relational diversity is _____

_____

D.	We need to look beyond the small stuff so we can see the whole person. An example of a time when I should not have sweat the small stuff is _____

_____

Additional Vocabulary

For each of the terms listed below, generate a personal example that illustrates the concept.

Friends of the heart _____

_____

Friends of the road _____

_____

Key Concepts

friends of the heart   relationship rules
friends of the road

Activities

Title	Individual	Partner	Group	Ethno.	Internet/InfoTrac
10.1 Styles of Friendship	✓		✓		
10.2 Features of Friendship	✓				
10.3 Relational Dialectics in Your Friendships	✓				✓
10.4 Why Friendships Wane	✓				
10.5 Long Distance Friendship	✓				
10.6 Long Distance Friendship and Technology	✓		✓		✓

Activity 10.1: Styles of Friendship

Purposes: To recognize different styles of experiencing and expressing closeness in friendships; To identify multiple styles of closeness in your friendships.

Instructions

1.   Identify a close friend of your sex and a second close friend of the other sex. Answer the questions on the form that appears on the next page for each friend.

2.   When you have completed your form, discuss features of friendship with others in your class. Are there common features that distinguish interaction in male-male, male-female, and female-female friendships?

Use the following scale to respond to questions about interaction in your friendships:

1 = occurs very often in the friendship

2 = occurs fairly often in the friendship

3 = occurs, but is not a regular feature of the friendship

4 = seldom occurs in the friendship

5 = never or virtually never occurs in the friendship

Type of Interaction	Same Sex Friend	Opposite Sex Friend
1. We talk about family issues and problems.		
2. We help each other out with repairs, loans, etc.		
3. We play sports together.		
4. We listen to each other's personal problems.		
5. We talk directly about our feelings for one another.		
6. We do things together like watching games, back packing, and going out to bars.		

Name _____

Activity 10.2: Features of Friendships

Purpose: To allow you to identify common features of friendship that operate in an important friendship.

Instructions

The form titled Features of Friendship focuses on five features that researchers have found are important in satisfying friendships in Western culture. If you wish to refresh your understanding of these features, review *Nature of Friendship* in the textbook.

Identify your closest friend. The friend may be your sex or the other sex as long as this is the person you regard as your closest friend. For each feature described on the form, indicate ways in which it is expressed and experienced in your friendship.

FEATURES OF FRIENDSHIP

Feature   *How expressed and experienced*

1. Willingness to invest in the friendship.

  * How do you invest?

  * How does your friend invest?

2. Intimacy

  * How do you express emotional closeness?

  * How important is closeness through dialogue?

  * How important is closeness through doing?

3. Acceptance

  * How do you let your friend know
    that you accept her/him, faults and all?

  * How does your friend demonstrate
    that she/he accepts you, faults and all?

4. Trust

  * Can you count on your friend to do
    what she/he says she/he will do?

  * Can your friend count on you to do
    what you say you will?

  * How does your friend show that she/he
    cares about you and your welfare?

  * How do you show your friend that you
    care about him/her and his/her welfare?

5. Support

  * How does your friend communicate that
    she/he supports you? Identify verbal and
    nonverbal forms of communication.

  * How do you communicate to your friend
    that you support her/him? Identify verbal and
    nonverbal forms of communication.

Name _____

Activity 10.3: Relational Dialectics in Your Friendships
(Using InfoTrac-College Edition)

Purposes: To heighten your awareness of the presence of relational dialectics in an important friendship in your life; To give you insight into the normalcy and health of opposing needs in a friendship of yours.

Instructions

1.   If you wish to refresh your understanding of relational dialectics, review *Internal Tensions* in the textbook.

2.   Identify an important friendship in your life. Using the form that appears on the next page, first provide an example from that friendship of each pole of the three relational dialectics. Second, identify what would be lost if the example you identified were not in your friendship.

Relational Dialectics in Your Friendship

Dialectic	Specific Example in your friendship	What would be lost if it were not present
Example		
Openness	I disclose to Jenetta about my worries about getting into graduate school	Jenetta would not know me well; I would not get her support

A. Autonomy/Connectedness

    A-1: Autonomy

    A-2: Connectedness

B. Novelty/Predictability

    B-1: Novelty

    B-2: Predictability

C. Openness/Closedness

    C-1: Openness

    C-2: Closedness

Search *InfoTrac-College Edition* keywords "friendship and work" to find articles that discuss tensions in relationships where co-workers are also friends. Bring ideas from these articles to share with the rest of your class.

Name _____

Activity 10.4: Why Friendships Wane

Purposes: To allow you to apply research discussed in the textbook to understand better friendships that have faded; To enhance your understanding of internal and external factors that can erode friendships in our lives.

Instructions: Identify a past friendship that was very important to you at one time, but that has waned or ended entirely. Check each of the statements on the form below that accurately describes that friendship when it was ending.

Signs of Waning Friendship

_____ 1.   My friend was less interested in getting together or talking with me.

_____ 2.   I was less interested in getting together or talking with my friend.

_____ 3.   Career demands took too much of my time.

_____ 4.   Career demands took too much of my friend's time.

_____ 5.   My family situation changed (I married, had or adopted a child, etc.).

_____ 6.   My friend's family situation changed.

_____ 7.   My friend violated my trust.

_____ 8.   I violated my friend's trust.

_____ 9.   My friend moved.

_____ 10.   I moved.

_____ 11.   There was sexual tension in the friendship.

_____ 12.   My friend's and my interests changed so that we no longer had strong common interests.

_____ 13.   I developed a new, strong friendship with another person.

_____ 14.   My friend developed a new, strong friendship with another person.

_____ 15.   The friendship became too routine and boring.

Name _____

Activity 10.5: Long Distance Friendship

Purposes: To allow you to apply research discussed in the textbook to a long distance friendship of yours; To increase your awareness of ways in which communication can ease the difficulty of sustaining a long distance friendship.

Instructions

1. Listed below are strategies for maintaining good communication in long distance friendships.

2. Identify a friend of yours who lives more than 60 miles away. Check each of the communication strategies listed below that you use to maintain the friendship.

3. For communication strategies that you are not now using, consider the value of including them in your friendship.

Use	Do Not Use	Communication Strategy
_____	_____	1. Call at least once a week.
_____	_____	2. Send electronic mail at least once a week.
_____	_____	3. Visit at least three times a year.
_____	_____	4. Write letters at least once a month.
_____	_____	5. Talk to the friend in your head.

Name _____

Activity 10.6: Long Distance Friendship and Technology
(Using the WWW)

<u>Purpose</u>: To learn about specific technologies long distance friends use to stay in touch with one another.

<u>Instructions</u>: Find three males and three females who actively maintain their relationship with friends over long distances. Create a series of questions to ask each person, including how long they have known each other, what technologies they use to stay in contact, advantages and disadvantages or challenges to maintaining their relationship, etc. Make a list of their answers and then see if you notice any patterns. For example, do people tend to use on type of technology more than another? Are there gender differences in the type of responses you collected?

<u>Questions To Ask</u>

1.

2.

3.

4.

5.

<u>People I Will Ask:</u>

Males	Females
1.	1.
2.	2.
3.	3.

<u>Patterns in Responses:</u>

Search *InfoTrac-College Edition* keywords "friendship and technology" to find articles on this topic. Are the findings of your informal research project consistent with other research discussed in these articles?

Using Your Everyday Encounters Premium Website

Use your *Everyday Encounters* premium website for quick access to the electronic study resources that accompany this text. The *Everyday Encounters* web site offers an interactive version of many of the activities in this chapter. You can complete these activities online and submit them electronically to your instructor. All of the web links included in this chapter as well as in the accompanying main text chapter are maintained on the web site, accessible through http://www.thomsonedu.com.

Included on the website is access to the Continuing the Conversation video scenario and questions featured in this chapter. Watch, listen to, and analyze the Continuing the Conversation case featuring *Sean and Bart* included at the end of Chapter 10 in your main text. The full transcript of Sean and Bart's conversation is included in your textbook. Watch, listen to and critique the conversation by completing the Conversation Analysis. You can compare your response to the authors by clicking on the Submit button at the end of the form.

Websites of Interest

The following URLs are maintained and updated on the *Everyday Encounters* web site, accessible through http://www.thomsonedu.com. We recommend you begin your web searches at this site to ensure that the links listed below are still active.

Name: Personal Relationships and Disabilities
Developer: Zana Marie Lutfiyya, Center on Human Policy, Syracuse University
Brief Description: The author discusses friendships between people with and without disabilities.
URL: http://soeweb.syr.edu/thechp/relshp.htm

Name: The Virtual Community
Developer: Howard Rheingold
Brief Description: This site contains an online version of Howard Rheingold's book *The Virtual Community* which discusses how people use computers to communicate, form friendships that serve as a basis for a community, and the tensions between "virtual" communities and "real" communities.
URL: http://www.rheingold.com/vc/book/

Name: Celebrate Friendship
Developer: Dave White
Brief Description: A list of books and resources about friendship and platonic love.
URL: http://www.celebratefriendship.org/

Name: Friendship
Developers: Dana, Brigette, Michelle, and Krissan, four students at Pleasant Grove Elementary School in Stockbridge, GA
Brief Description: Includes information on what kids say about friendship, friendship poems, and how to be a good friend from the perspective of pre-teens.
URL: http://www.henry.k12.ga.us/pges/instruction/kid-pages/friendship/default.html

Name: Friendship Compatibility Quiz
Developer: iVillage
Brief Description: A questionnaire for friends to complete together (asynchronously or in real time) and compare results to identify their degree of compatibility based on communication style, priorities, or relationship style.
URL: http://www.ivillage.com/Insquizfnf/topics/0,,4tg2,00.html?ics=ivk,searcht

Name: Office Friendships Can Boost the Bottom Line
Developer: John Burke, Bankrate.com
Brief Description: Reports on Gallup survey that found good friends in the workplace can have a positive effect on employee motivation and job satisfaction.
URL: http://www.bankrate.com/brm/news/biz/thumb/20011128a.asp?prodtype=biz

Self Test

Multiple Choice

_____ 1. _____ speech communities emphasize closeness through dialogue.

    A. Urban
    B. Feminine
    C. Masculine
    D. Workplace

_____ 2. Closeness through doing involves:

    A. responsive and supportive communication.
    B. talk as the primary pathway to intimacy.
    C. messages that are disclosing and emotionally expressive.
    D. sharing activities.

_____ 3. Men often provide support to their friends through:

    A.   covert intimacy.
    B.   verbal emotional support.
    C.   talking about fears that arise in stressful situations.
    D.   identifying and venting feelings.

_____ 4. When friends assume that the relationship will continue even if they don't have specific dates in mind, the stage of friendship they are experiencing is:

    A.   waning friendship.
    B.   stabilized friendship.
    C.   nascent friendship.
    D.   friendly relations.

_____ 5. The reason that a majority of high school friendships dissolve when friends go to college is which of the following?

    A.   Each person finds new friends.
    B.   Geographic distance hinders interaction.
    C.   Each person develops new interests.
    D.   Education changes people.

_____ 6. In adulthood, friendships are:

    A.   primarily with members of the other sex.
    B.   central to an individual's self-worth.
    C.   more difficult to sustain.
    D.   less important than in other stages of life.

True/False

_____ 7. Instrumental activities are the cornerstone of feminine speech communities.

_____ 8. Even when students leave home for college, their families still remain the first people they turn to for help and support.

_____ 9. Our economic status affects both who we choose as friends and whether the relationship can be sustained by long-distance.

_____ 10. Lack of interaction is more damaging to best friendships than casual friendships.

11. Differences between how women and men create and express closeness are more matters of degree than absolute contrasts.

_____ 12. Relationships maintained through face-to-face contact are more personal and committed than those maintained through e-mail and the internet.

Essay

13. Describe how diverse communication styles may both complicate and enrich friendships.

14. Identify and describe five features of close friendships among most Westerners.

15. List and discuss the guidelines for communication between friends.

Personal Reflections

1. Describe a friendship you have with a member of your sex. Analyze the extent to which it conforms to the gender patterns described in the text.

2. Describe a friendship you have with a member of the other sex. Analyze the extent to which it conforms to the gender patterns described in the text.

3. Review the research on rules of friendship covered in Chapter 10 of your textbook. Analyze how these rules affect or don't pertain to your friendships. Are there other rules specific to your friendships?

4. Consider a friendship that you sustain over long distances. What technologies (e.g., phone, e-mail, e-Cards, web pages, chat rooms, video phones, etc.) do you use to sustain this relationship? Do you use different technologies for different kinds of communication activities?

Chapter 11: Committed Romantic Relationships

I. Committed romantic relationships are voluntary, involve I-Thou communication, include sexual and romantic feelings, and are considered primary and permanent in our society.

   A. Our traditional definition of two heterosexual parents and children has evolved to include a variety of romantic relationship configurations both here and around the world.

   B. Generally, romantic love involves passion (intensely positive feelings and desires for another person), commitment (an intention to remain in the relationship), and intimacy (feelings of connection, closeness, and tenderness).

   C. Romantic relationships develop based upon the love styles the partners exhibit.

      1. There are three primary love styles.

         a. Eros is an intense love that usually includes early self disclosure, sentimental expressions, and a quick falling in love period.

         b. Storge love grows out of friendship and is usually characterized by stability.

         c. Those who exhibit a ludus style view love as a game that usually includes adventure, puzzles, and commitment avoidance.

      2. There are three secondary love styles.

        a.   <u>Pragma</u> combines storge and ludus love styles; people who exhibit this love style usually have clear criteria for partners that must be met before they fall in love.

        b.   <u>Mania</u> combines eros and ludus love styles; people who exhibit this love style usually devise games and tests for their potential partners and experience emotional extremes.

        c.   <u>Agape</u> combines eros and storge love styles; people who exhibit this love style usually put another's happiness ahead of their own without any expectation of reciprocity.

II.   Like friendships, romantic relationships in Western societies tend to follow a relatively predictable path.

    A.   <u>Growth</u> stages begin a romantic relationship.

        1.   We are <u>individuals</u> before we ever meet our potential romantic partner.

        2.   <u>Invitational communication</u> is where we indicate to the other person that we are interested in interacting. One way I indicate interest is _____

        _____

        3.   <u>Explorational communication</u> involves considering the possibilities for a long-term relationship. One way I explore in a committed romantic relationship is

        _____

4. <u>Intensifying communication</u> occurs when we express more personal thoughts and feelings as well as begin to create our own relational culture. At this point in a committed romantic relationship, I usually express _____

_____

5. <u>Revising communication</u> indicates the possible problems and dissatisfactions that exist within the relationship as well as evaluates the likelihood of the relationship continuing.

6. <u>Commitment</u> involves the decision to stay with the relationship over the long haul and arrange other aspects of their lives around this relationship. I have expressed commitment in a romantic relationship by_____

_____

B. <u>Navigation</u> maintains a relationship by adjusting, working through new problems, revisiting old problems, and accommodating changes in both individual and relational lives.

1. <u>Relational culture</u> is the private world of rules, understandings, meanings, and patterns of acting and interpreting that partners create and agree upon for their relationship. Examples of relational culture I have experienced or witnessed are

_____

and _____

2. In <u>placemaking</u> we create an environment that indicates our relationship as well as what we value, experience, and like. An example of placemaking I have experienced or witnessed is _____

_____

256

C.   Deterioration stages signal a possible end to a romantic relationship.

  1.   In the <u>intrapsychic</u> phase, we focus on perceived declines in closeness/intimate communication or lapses in joint activities/acts of consideration.

  2.   Dyadic breakdown occurs when romantic partners gradually stop engaging in their established patterns, understandings, and routines that make up their relational culture.

  3.   <u>Social support</u> occurs when we look to others to help us get through the relationship's breakdown. For social support I would turn to _____.

  4.   <u>Grave dressing</u> is burying the relationship and accepting that it has come to a close.

  5.   <u>Resurrection</u> process occurs when both partners go on with the lives without the other as an intimate.

IV.   Communicating in committed, healthy, romantic relationships requires an understanding of four guidelines

  A.   Engaging in <u>dual perspective</u> lets your partner know that you understand her/his perspective and that you take into consideration when communicating.

  B.   With the rise of HIV/AIDS comes the responsibility of talking about and <u>practicing safer sex</u>, two things we are not always comfortable talking about or doing.

  C.   Manage conflict constructively as violence and abuse among romantic partners are, unfortunately, more common than we think.

  D.   Adapt communication to the unique needs of partners in commuter relationships.

Additional Vocabulary

For each of the terms listed below, generate a personal example that illustrates the concept.

Passion _____

_____

Intimacy _____

_____

Eros _____

_____

Storge _____

_____

Ludus _____

_____

Pragma _____

_____

Mania _____

_____

Agape _____

_____

Revising communication _____

_____

_____

Navigating _____

_____

Intrapsychic phase _____

_____

Grave dressing _____

_____

Environmental Spoiling _____

_____

Key Concepts

agape
committed romantic relationships
committment
environmental spoiling
eros
intimacy
ludus

mania
passion
placemaking
pragma
relational culture
storge

Activities

Title	Individual	Partner	Group	Ethno.	Internet/InfoTrac
11.1 Let's Get Personal	✓				✓
11.2 The Music of Love	✓				✓
11.3 Recognizing Styles of Love	✓				
11.4 Identifying Stages in Romantic Relationships	✓				
11.5 Relational Dialectics in Your Romantic Relationships	✓				
11.6 On-line Dating Services and Diversity	✓				✓

Name _____

Activity 11.1: Let's Get Personal
(Using the WWW)

Purposes: To increase your awareness of the bases of romantic attraction in our era; To increase your sensitivity to differences in criteria for romantic partners that are used by heterosexual women, heterosexual men, lesbians, and gay men.

Instructions

1.   Obtain one or more state-wide newspapers or other publications that include a large section of personals ads. Alternatively, you can use online personal advertisements (start with your favorite search engine and type in "online personal ads"). You should have a large enough sample of ads to have at least 10 ads each for: men seeking men, men seeking women, women seeking men, and women seeking women.

2.   Use the four forms that follow this page to record the criteria specified by ad-writers when they describe desirable romantic partners.

3.   Compare trends in the criteria used by the four groups of individuals.

Form for Analyzing Personal Ads by Men for Men

Ad #	Physical Qualities	Personal Qualities	Career Success	Interest in Talk	Activities	Financial Resources
1.						
2.						
3.						
4.						
5.						
6.						
7.						
8.						
9.						
10.						

Form for Analyzing Personal Ads by Men for Women

Ad #	Physical Qualities	Personal Qualities	Career Success	Interest in Talk	Activities	Financial Resources
1.						
2.						
3.						
4.						
5.						
6.						
7.						
8.						
9.						
10.						

Form for Analyzing Personal Ads by Women for Men

Ad #	Physical Qualities	Personal Qualities	Career Success	Interest in Talk	Activities	Financial Resources
1.						
2.						
3.						
4.						
5.						
6.						
7.						
8.						
9.						
10.						

Form for Analyzing Personal Ads by Women for Women

Ad #	Physical Qualities	Personal Qualities	Career Success	Interest in Talk	Activities	Financial Resources
1.						
2.						
3.						
4.						
5.						
6.						
7.						
8.						
9.						
10.						

Name _____

Activity 11.2: The Music of Love
(Using the WWW)

Purposes: To identify stages of romantic relationships in popular music; To understand better how stages of romance are experienced and expressed in popular communication.

Instructions

1. If you wish to refresh your knowledge of different stages that are commonly experienced in the development of romantic relationships, review *The Development of Romantic Relationships* in the textbook.

2. This activity invites you to identify stages of romance that are emphasized in currently popular songs. Using the form titled The Music of Love, identify a current or recent popular song that reflects each stage in romantic relationships.

3. Quote specific lyrics in the song that lead you to associate that song with a particular stage in romantic relationships. To find complete lyrics for particular songs, visit http://www.lyrics.com or http://www.azlyrics.com.

4. When you have completed the form, notice which stages of romantic relationships you either could not find a song to represent or you had difficulty finding an appropriate song. What does this tell you about which phases of romance are most celebrated in popular culture?

The Music of Love

Stage	Song	Specific Lyrics
Intensifying	Near You (by Alison Krauss)	"Love you whenever we're together; love you when we're apart." "The things you do endear you to me."
Individual Characteristics		
Invitational Communication		
Explorational Communication		

267

Intensifying Communication (Euphoria)		
5. Revising Communication		
Commitment		
Navigating		
Intrapsychic Phase		

Dyadic Processes		
Social Support		
Grave Dressing		
Resurrection Process		

Name _____

Activity 11.3: Recognizing Styles of Love

Purpose: To give you experience in identifying communication that reflects particular styles of loving.

Instructions

1.   If you wish to refresh your knowledge of the different styles of love, review *Styles of Loving* in the textbook.

2.   Listed below 15 statements that might be made by a person about romance or a romantic partner. Identify the style of love reflected in each of the statements (eros, storge, ludus, pragma, mania, agape).

3.   Answers appear at the end of the chapter.

Style of Love	Statement
Example	
Agape	Your happiness is my happiness.
_____	1. I want to tell my partner everything about me as soon as I fall in love.
_____	2. My partner is my best friend.
_____	3. I could only fall in love with someone of my race and class.
_____	4. I am looking for a partner who will be a good parent.
_____	5. Love's a game–I never take it too seriously.

_____ 6.   I wish I could be sure Pat loves me. I worry all the time.

_____ 7.   I put Kim's welfare and desires ahead of my own, and that's the way I want it to be.

_____ 8.   I fall in love hard and fast.

_____ 9.   I am not looking for a committed relationship, just some fun.

_____ 10. All I can think about is this relationship. Nothing and nobody else matters to me.

_____ 11. I am happiest when my partner is happy.

_____ 12. What I like best about my relationship is that it is so steady and peaceful–none of those dramatic ups and downs that some couples have.

_____ 13. I need to make sure my partner loves me, so I come up with tests a lot of the time.

_____ 14. I intend to marry someone who is professionally ambitious.

_____ 15. Our love just grew very gradually. We started off as friends, and eventually romantic interest developed an extra layer on the basic foundation of friendship.

Name _____

Activity 11.4: Identifying Stages in Romantic Relationships

Purpose: To give you experience in identifying communication that reflects different stages in the evolution of romantic relationships.

Instructions

1.   If you wish to refresh your knowledge of the different stages in the evolution of romantic relationships, *The Organization of Romantic Relationships* in the textbook.

2.   Listed below are 12 interactions between partners A and B that would be most likely to occur at specific stages in a romantic relationship.

3.   Identify the stage of romance most clearly reflected in each of the interactions.

4.   Answers appear at the end of the chapter.

Stage	Interaction Between Partners
Revising	A: Before I could consider a permanent relationship, you would need to stop smoking.
	B: I understand that condition.
1. _____	A: Where are you from?
	B: Ohio. Where is your home?
2. _____	A: I plan to spend the rest of my life with you.
	B: I feel the same way.
3. _____	A: (thought, not stated) I'm just not happy in this relationship. We don't communicate any more.
	B: (thought, not stated) I really miss doing things together.

4. _____ A: Do you enjoy bands like this one?

B: Sure, but I like jazz even more. Do you like jazz?

5. _____ A: I think I finally understand what went wrong in our relationship and why we couldn't make it work.

B: Me too, so now we can let it go.

6. _____ A: It's so comfortable to have established routines and understandings in our relationship.

B: Yeah, there's a nice basic rhythm in our lives together.

7. _____ A: I just called to say good night. Even though we spent 4 hours just talking tonight, I wanted to talk to you once more before going to sleep.

B: I'm glad you called. I can't get enough of you.

8. _____ A: (unstated realization) We don't ask about each other's day anymore like we used to do all the time.

B: (unstated realization) We used to go out for brunch every Sunday, but we don't any more.

9. _____ A: (to parent) It's over between Pat and me, and I'm really sad.

B: (to friend) Kim and I just broke up and I'm kind of down.

10. _____ A: I know that I love you, but I'm not sure we can make a permanent life together.

B: Why not? Let's talk about your questions and see if we can find answers to them. I want to make this work.

11. _____ A: How are we going to tell our parents we're separating? There's never been a divorce in either of our families.

B: I know. I think it's really important that neither of us blame each other when we talk to our families. Will you agree to that?

Name _____

Activity 11.5: Relational Dialectics in Your Romantic Relationship

Purposes: To heighten your awareness of the presence of relational dialectics in an important current or past romantic relationship in your life; To give you insight into the normalcy and health of opposing needs in a current or past romantic relationship in which you are or have been involved.

Instructions

1.   If you wish to refresh your understanding of relational dialectics, review *Navigating* in the textbook.

2.   Identify an important current or past romantic relationship in your life. Use that relationship as the referent for responding to the form on the following page. Use the form below to provide an example of each pole of the three relational dialectics.

3.   Identify what would be lost if the example you identified weas not in your romantic relationship.

Relational Dialectics in Your Romantic Relationship

Dialectic	Specific Example in your relationship	What would be lost if this were not present
Example		
Autonomy	I spend most weekends in a private retreat so that I can write without interference.	I would be unhappy if I did not have time to write. I would not appreciate time with Robbie as much if it were routine.

A. Autonomy/Connectedness

    A-1: Autonomy

    A-2: Connectedness

Dialectic	Specific Example in your relationship	What would be lost if this were not present
Example		
Autonomy	I spend most weekends in a private retreat so that I can write without interference.	I would be unhappy if I did not have time to write. I would not appreciate time with Robbie as much if it were routine.

B. Novelty/Predictability

   B-1: Novelty

   B-2: Predictability

C. Openness/Closedness

   C-1: Openness

   C-2: Closedness

Name _____

Activity 11.6: On-line Dating Services and Diversity (Using the WWW)

Purpose: To analyze similarities and differences in web-based dating services targeting diverse populations.

Instructions: Go to your favorite web search engine (such as AltaVista or Google) and search for web pages devoted to online dating services. Find at least three online dating services that target diverse populations, such as "Christian Dating Services," "Jewish Dating Services," "Asian Dating Services," "Gay Dating Services," etc. Visit these three web sites and record any similarities and differences among the sites.

Web Site #1

Web Site #2

Web Site #3

Similarities

Differences

Answers to Activity 11.3 Recognizing Styles of Love

1.   Eros
2.   Storge
3.   Pragma
4.   Pragma
5.   Ludus
6.   Mania
7.   Agape
8.   Eros
9.   Ludus
10.   Mania
11.   Agape
12.   Storge
13.   Mania
14.   Pragma
15.   Storge

Answers to Activity 11.4 Identifying Stages in Romantic Relationships

1.   Invitational communication
2.   Commitment
3.   Intrapsychic phase
4.   Explorational communication
5.   Grave dressing
6.   Navigating
7.   Intensifying communication (euphoria)
8.   Dyadic processes
9.   Social support
10.   Revising communication
11.   Resurrection processes

Using Your Everyday Encounters Premium Website

Use your *Everyday Encounters* premium website for quick access to the electronic study resources that accompany this text. The *Everyday Encounters* web site offers an interactive version of many of the activities in this chapter. You can complete these activities online and submit them electronically to your instructor. All of the web links included in this chapter as well as in the accompanying main text chapter are maintained on the web site, accessible through http://www.thomsonedu.com.

Included on the website is access to the Continuing the Conversation video scenario and questions featured in this chapter. Watch, listen to, and analyze the Continuing the Conversation case featuring *Meg and Trevor* included at the end of Chapter 11 in your main text. The full transcript of Meg and Trevor's conversation is included in your textbook. Watch, listen to and critique the conversation by completing the Conversation Analysis. You can compare your response to the authors by clicking on the Submit button at the end of the form.

Websites of Interest

The following URLs are maintained and updated on the *Everyday Encounters* web site, accessible through http://www.thomsonedu.com. We recommend you begin your web searches at this site to ensure that the links listed below are still active.

Name: Talking To Your Partner About Condom Use
Developer: Mary Elizabeth McKenna, University of Massachusetts at Lowell
Brief Description: This web page provides a table of what to say to a partner in negotiating using a condom (e.g., If your partner says... You say...).
URL: http://www.uml.edu/student-services/counseling/condom/index.html

Name: A-Z Lyrics Universe
Developer: AZLyrics.com
Brief Description: Browse by artist, or search using artist's name, album title, or song title.
URL: http://www.azlyrics.com/

Name: Lyrics.com
Developer: Lyrics.com
Brief Description: This web site contains lyrics to popular songs organized by artist.
URL: http://www.lyrics.com

Name: La Chaise Longue
Developer: Queendom.com
Brief Description: This web site is similar to a "Dear Abby" column but has some good points about various relationship topics.

URL: http://queendom.com/chaiselongue/

Name: Healthy Relationships
Developer: Youth Resource
Brief Description: Includes articles, stories, a comparison of healthy and unhealthy relationships, and a link to the website's section on dating violence.
URL: http://www.youthresource.com/our_lives/dating_violence

Name: Jewish Dating Revolutionized
Developer: Aish HaTorah
Brief Description: This site provides a series of articles, advice, and journal reflections about dating from a Jewish perspective.
URL: http://aish.com/dating/

Name: Long Distance Relationships
Developer: Geraldine Voost
Brief Description: This site provides tips for negotiating long distance relationships.
URL: http://www.etoile.co.uk/Love/Long.html

Name: Same Sex Marriage: A Selective Bibliography
Developer: Paul Axel-Lute, Rutgers Law Library, Newark
Brief Description: An extensive bibliography addressing all views on the issues, including international debates and laws.
URL: http://law-library.rutgers.edu/SSM.html

Name: Domestic/Dating Violence
Developer: Counseling Center, University of Massachusetts at Lowell
Brief Description: This web page provides resources and links on domestic violence.
URL: http://www.uml.edu/student-services/counseling/violence/index.html

Name: Lovestories.com
Developer: Lovestories.com
Brief Description: This commercial web site includes poems, journals, and stories devoted to love.
URL: http://www.lovestories.com

Self Test

Multiple Choice

_____ 1. Commitment:

    A.   happens without effort.
    B.   is a relationship choice.
    C.   focuses on the present moment.
    D.   fades in the face of disappointment and troubles.

_____ 2. Which one of the following is NOT a primary style of love?

    A.   eros
    B.   pragma
    C.   storge
    D.   ludus

_____ 3. Mary says, "There's nothing I wouldn't do for Kirk. All I want is for him to be happy and be able to pursue his dreams. If he can do that, I'll be happy too." Mary seems to be experiencing _____ love.

    A.   ludic
    B.   erotic
    C.   manic
    D.   agapic

_____ 4. The private world of rules, understandings, meanings, and patterns of acting and interpreting each other that intimate partners create is called:

    A.   placemaking.
    B.   relational horizon.
    C.   relational culture.
    D.   navigational norms.

_____ 5. One of the reasons given in the textbook for neglecting safe sex precautions is

    A.   being incapacitated by drugs or alcohol
    B.   the risk of STD is low
    C.   the time involved with communicating about safe sex
    D.   new HIV cases are rapidly decreasing due to publicity about the dangers of AIDS

_____ 6. When meeting someone new, which of the following is NOT an influence on initial interaction?

A. self-concept
B. similarity
C. chronemics
D. proximity

True/False

_____ 7. Men and women perceive the goal of the first date to be companionship.

_____ 8. Ludic lovers enjoy an even keeled friendship based on relationships.

_____ 9. Explorational communication focuses on exchanging information and includes some self-disclosure.

_____ 10. Revising communication is the stage in developing relationships in which partners clarify their messages for better understanding.

_____ 11. Many intimate, committed couples find talking about sex to be embarrassing.

_____ 12. Shy or apprehensive people report that computer dating services can help when interacting with others.

Essay

12. Describe and give an example of navigating in committed romantic relationships. Include the concepts relational culture and placemaking in your answer.

13. Identify how various communication technologies can be used to deal with challenges (or difficulties) in maintaining long distance romantic relationships.

Personal Reflections

1. Describe a current or past romantic relationship in terms of the stages of romance discussed in your textbook. Analyze the extent to which your relationship followed or deviated from the typical pattern identified in the text. If it did not follow the "standard" pattern, explain why you think it did not.

2. If you are in a long distance relationship, explain how communication in it differs from a romantic relationship in which you and your partner are geographically together.

Chapter 12:   Communication in Families

I.   One of the most notable features of families is their diversity.

     A.   The forms families take today very greatly. Examples of diverse forms of families I
know include_____

_____

_____

_____

     B.   The goals for being in a long term commitment vary today.

          1. Some couples are looking for "individualized relationships." An example of this is a
couple I know_____

          2.   More women work out of the home today than in past decades.

          3. The idea of marriage varies across cultures. One couple I know who views marriage
differently than Western culture is_____

          4. Relationships follow typically one of three paths toward commitment including
gradual progression, rapid escalation, and medium-length courtship.

II.   There are at least three ways we indicate that we are involved in a long-term, committed,
romantic relationship.

     A.   Cohabitation occurs when two romantic partners decide to live together, either before
they get married or in place of getting married. _____ and

_____ are two people I know who are cohabiting.

B.   Gay and lesbian commitments, sometimes in the form of ceremonies, frequently precede living together. _____ and _____ are two people I know in a committed gay/lesbian relationship.

C.   Marriage is still the most popular way of publicly showing our romantic, committed connection to another person.

    1.   While almost everyone expects to get married in their lifetime, there are a variety of paths we can take to get there and a variety of ways we can view the marriage once we are in it.

    2.   Different relationship researchers have identified distinct classification systems of various types of marriages.

    3.   Words (process of communicating), thoughts (how we think about each other and the marriage), and emotions all influence how satisfied we are with our marriage.

III.   The typical life cycle of families with children generally includes seven steps: establishing a family, enlarging a family, developing a family, encouraging independence, launching children, post-launching of children, and retirement.

IV.   Three distinct types of marriage are known to exist.

A.   <u>Traditionals</u> are known to be_____ and _____.

B.   <u>Independents</u> are known to be_____

and _____

and _____.

    C.   <u>Separates</u> are the most common type of relationship, and they are known to be _____

_____.

V.   In addition to the guidelines presented previously, committed romantic relationships have four guidelines for making them more effective.

    A.   Partners need to strive to maintain equity, or fairness, in family relationships. An example of a time when I felt an unequal level of responsibility is_____

_____

    B.   Partners need to demonstrate that they value and respect one another for who they are and not for who we would like them to be. An example of a time when I should have shown more respect and value for my partner is _____

_____

    C.   We need to overlook the small frustrations and irritations that crop up in our relationships. An example of a time when I should not have sweat the small stuff is ___

_____

    D.   Make daily choices that enhance the intimacy we have in our relationships. An example of a time when I should have worked harder at the day-to-day aspects of my romantic relationship is _____

_____

Additional Vocabulary

For each of the terms listed below, generate a personal example that illustrates the concept.

Individualized relationships _____

_____

Social Exchange Theory _____

_____

Psychological responsibility _____

_____

Key Concepts

equity   second shift
psychological responsibility   social exchange theory

Activities

Title	Individual	Partner	Group	Ethno.	Internet/InfoTrac
12.1 Learning about All Types of Relationships	X				X
12.2 The Music of Family	X	X			X

Name _____

Activity 12.1: Learning About Diverse Relationships
(Using the WWW)

<u>Purposes</u>: To increase your awareness of committed relationships of all kinds. To increase your sensitivity to differences in criteria for romantic partners that are used by heterosexual women, heterosexual men, lesbians, and gay men.

<u>Instructions</u>

1. Obtain one or more state-wide newspapers or other publications that include a large section of personals ads. Alternatively, you can use online personal advertisements (start with your favorite search engine and type in "online personal ads"). You should have a large enough sample of ads to have at least 10 ads each for: men seeking men, men seeking women, women seeking men, and women seeking women.

2. Use the four forms that follow this page to record the criteria specified by ad-writers when they describe desirable romantic partners.

3. Compare trends in the criteria used by the four groups of individuals.

Form for Analyzing Personal Ads by Men for Men

Ad #	Physical Qualities	Personal Qualities	Career Success	Interest in Talk	Activities	Financial Resources
1.						
2.						
3.						
4.						
5.						
6.						
7.						
8.						
9.						
10.						

Form for Analyzing Personal Ads by Men for Women

Ad #	Physical Qualities	Personal Qualities	Career Success	Interest in Talk	Activities	Financial Resources
1.						
2.						
3.						
4.						
5.						
6.						
7.						
8.						
9.						
10.						

Form for Analyzing Personal Ads by Women for Men

Ad #	Physical Qualities	Personal Qualities	Career Success	Interest in Talk	Activities	Financial Resources
1.						
2.						
3.						
4.						
5.						
6.						
7.						
8.						
9.						
10.						

Form for Analyzing Personal Ads by Women for Women

Ad #	Physical Qualities	Personal Qualities	Career Success	Interest in Talk	Activities	Financial Resources
1.						
2.						
3.						
4.						
5.						
6.						
7.						
8.						
9.						
10.						

Name _____

Activity 12.2: The Music of Love
(Using the WWW)

<u>Purposes</u>: To identify family stages in popular music; To understand better how stages of the family cycle.

<u>Instructions</u>

1. If you wish to refresh your knowledge of different stages that are commonly experienced in the development of romantic relationships, review *The Family Life Cycle* in the textbook.

2. Quote specific lyrics in the song that lead you to associate that song with a particular stage in the family cycle. To find complete lyrics for particular songs, visit http://www.lyrics.com or http://www.azlyrics.com.

3. Compare your findings with your classmates. How did the music genre represent the stages?

Using Your Everyday Encounters Premium Website

Use your *Everyday Encounters* premium website for quick access to the electronic study resources that accompany this text. The *Everyday Encounters* web site offers an interactive version of many of the activities in this chapter. You can complete these activities online and submit them electronically to your instructor. All of the web links included in this chapter as well as in the accompanying main text chapter are maintained on the web site, accessible through http://www.thomsonedu.com.

Included on the website is access to the Continuing the Conversation video scenario and questions featured in this chapter. Watch, listen to, and analyze the Continuing the Conversation case featuring *Dan and Charlotte* included at the end of Chapter 12 in your main text. The full transcript of Dan and Charlotte's conversation is included in your textbook. Watch, listen to and critique the conversation by completing the Conversation Analysis. You can compare your response to the authors by clicking on the Submit button at the end of the form.

Websites of Interest

The following URLs are maintained and updated on the *Everyday Encounters* web site, accessible through http://www.thomsonedu.com. We recommend you begin your web searches at this site to ensure that the links listed below are still active.

Name: All Acts of Love and Pleasure: Promiscuity, Romance, and Respect
Developer: Columbine's Laboratory
Brief Description: This web page discusses the importance of being honest about what we are seeking in romantic relationships.
URL: http://apocalypse.org/pub/u/hilda/lnpart.html

Name: Making Committed Relationships Work
Developer: Institute of Agriculture and Natural Resources
Brief Description: This web page provides a set of views on how to make committed relationships work (communication is at the heart of the recommendations).
URL: http://ianrwww.unl.edu/ianr/fcs/efrfeb97.htm

Name: The Effects Of Parental Divorce On Adult Children's Romantic Relationships
Developer: Hope College Psychology Department
Brief Description: A short thought piece on the effects divorce has on the children when they grow up and enter romantic relationships.
URL: http://www.hope.edu/academic/psychology/335/webrep2/divorce.html

Name: Lesbian.com

Developer: Lesbian.com
Brief Description: A directory for the lesbian, gay, bisexual, and transgendered community, the site also includes links to sites based on "how we identify," such as deaf lesbians, dykes with disabilities, and lesbians of color.
URL: http://www.lesbian.com

Name: Gay.com
Developer: Gay.com
Brief Description: Available in several languages, this website includes information on relationships, health, careers, travel, and entertainment for the gay, lesbian, bisexual, and transgendered community.
URL: http://www.gay.com

Self Test

Multiple Choice

_____ 1. Historically Americans have viewed the goal of marriage to be

    A.   lifelong partners
    B.   raising children
    C.   a financial arrangement
    D.   individualized relationships

_____ 2. The second stage in family life may be a time of adjusting expectations while experiencing some disappointments. This stage is called

    A.   establishing a family.
    B.   encouraging independence.
    C.   postlaunching of children.
    D.   enlarging a family.

_____ 3. Equity theory states that partners perceive the relationship as

    A.   equitable over time.
    B.   sharing in household responsibilities.
    C.   social exchange theory.
    D.   providing moment-to-moment equality.

_____ 4. The most common family form involves

A.   two same-sex partners.
B.   marriage and cohabitation.
C.   agapic love.
D.   children.

_____ 5.   Satisfying communication in long-term commitments includes three key elements which are

A.   thoughts, moods, and attitudes.
B.   facts, feelings, and climate.
C.   words, thoughts, and emotions.
D.   equity, exchange, and equality.

True/False

_____ 6.   Fathers' communication appears to be a strong influence on children's self-esteem.

_____ 7.   In some cultures arranged marriages are common today.

_____ 8.   Psychological responsibility involves doing the physical tasks involved in shopping, cleaning, and caring for children.

_____ 9.   Different pathways toward marriage may reflect partners' love styles.

_____ 10.   While distinct types of marriages exist, a couple will stay fixed in one during the course of their relationship.

_____ 11.   The highest level of martial satisfaction occurs in the independent marriages.

_____ 12.   After children leave the home, partners must redefine their marriage.

Essay

13.   Describe and give an example of partners you know who have satisfying relationships due to their communication which includes words, thoughts, and emotions.

14.   Define equity in relationships and discuss the consequences of inequity (both being over benefited and being under benefited)..

Personal Reflections

1.   Describe a current or past romantic relationship in terms of the paths to commitment discussed in your textbook. Analyze the extent to which your relationship followed or deviated from the typical path identified in the text. If it did not follow the "standard" pattern, explain why you think it did not.

2.   Consider the advantages and disadvantages of meeting someone on-line for a potential romantic relationship. If you have never met someone on-line, consider why you have not.

Self Test Answers

Chapter 1

1.	D	(p.11)
2.	D	(p.19)
3.	B	(p.38)
4.	B	(p.39)
5.	A	(p.18)
6.	D	(p.31)
7.	True	(p.29)
8.	True	(p.21)
9.	False	(p.27)
10.	False	(p.27)
11.	False	(p.30)
12.	True	(p.27)

Chapter 2

1.	C	(p.45)
2.	C	(p.52)
3.	A	(p.47)
4.	A	(p.58)
5.	B	(p.44)
6.	C	(p.53)
7.	D	(p.48)
8.	False	(p.45)
9.	True	(p.63)
10.	False	(p.63)
11.	False	(p.59)
12.	False	(p.45)

Chapter 3

1.	C	(p.79)
2.	B	(p.81)
3.	A	(p.75)
4.	B	(p.76)
5.	A	(p.83-89)
6.	True	(p.73)
7.	True	(p.75)
8.	False	(p.87)
9.	True	(p.74)
10.	False	(p.81)
11.	False	(p.80)

Chapter 4

1.	D	(p.107)
2.	B	(p.108)
3.	A	(p.108)
4.	C	(p.111)
5.	C	(p.115)
6.	D	(p.106)
7.	False	(p.122)
8.	True	(p.122)
9.	False	(p.117)
10.	False	(p.126)
11.	True	(p.103)
12.	True	(p.110)

Chapter 5

1.	C	(p.136-137)
2.	B	(p.140)
3.	C	(p.135)
4.	D	(p.134)
5.	A	(p.149)
6.	B	(p.148)
7.	True	(p.138)
8.	True	(p.137)
9.	False	(p.136)
10.	True	(p.150)
11.	True	(p.151-152)
12.	True	(p.136)

Chapter 6

1.	C	(p.166)
2.	D	(p.168)
3.	A	(p.173)
4.	D	(p.171)
5.	C	(p.179)
6.	B	(p.176)
7.	True	(p.162)
8.	False	(p.163)
9.	True	(p.168)
10.	False	(p.164)
11.	True	(p.161)
12.	False	(p.171)

Chapter 7
1. D (p.191)
2. D (p.196)
3. A (p.196)
4. C (p.197)
5. B (p.190)
6. True (p.198)
7. True (p.190)
8. True (p.198)
9. False (p.198)
10. True (p.201)
11. True (p.198)
12, False (p.186)

Chapter 8
1. A (p.216)
2. A (p.217)
3. D (p.215)
4. C (p.223)
5. A (p.225)
6. A (p.232)
7. C (p.219)
8. True (p.217)
9. False (p.224)
10. True (p.225)
11. True (p.237)
12. False (p.221)

Chapter 9
1. D (p.244)
2. A (p.250)
3. B (p.251)
4. B (p.253)
5. A (p.245)
6. B (p.256)
7. False (p.257)
8. True (p.246)
9. True (p.243)
10. False (p.244)
11. False (p.247)
12. False (p.264)

Chapter 10
1. B (p.274-275)
2. D (p.275)
3. A (p.279)
4. B (p.282)
5. B (p.288)
6. C (p.287)
7. False (p.276)
8. False (p.279)
9. True (p.288)
10. False (p.282)
11. True (p.276)
12. False (p.282)

Chapter 11
1. B (p.299)
2. B (p.301)
3. D (p.303)
4. C (p.308)
5. A (p.313)
6. C (p.305)
7. False (p.304)
8. False (p.301)
9. True (p.306)
10. False (p.307)
11. True (p.313)
12. True (p.306)

Chapter 12
1. B (p.324)
2. D (p.333)
3. A (p.339)
4. B (p.323)
5. C (p.331)
6. True (p.335)
7. True (p.325)
8. False (p.340)
9. True (p.326)
10. False (p.329)
11. False (p.329)
12. True (p.337)